Responsible Care in a Post-Roe World

Responsible Care in a Post-Roe World

The Impacts and Ethical Responsibilities of Mental Health Professionals

Jennifer Toof

Ami Crowley

BLOOMSBURY ACADEMIC

NEW YORK · LONDON · OXFORD · NEW DELHI · SYDNEY

BLOOMSBURY ACADEMIC
Bloomsbury Publishing Inc, 1359 Broadway, New York, NY 10018, USA
Bloomsbury Publishing Plc, 50 Bedford Square, London, WC1B 3DP, UK
Bloomsbury Publishing Ireland, 29 Earlsfort Terrace, Dublin 2, D02 AY28, Ireland

BLOOMSBURY, BLOOMSBURY ACADEMIC and the Diana logo are trademarks of
Bloomsbury Publishing Plc

First published in the United States of America 2025

Library of Congress Cataloging-in-Publication Data is available

ISBN: HB: 978-1-5381-9431-7
PB: 978-1-5381-9432-4
ePDF: 979-8-8818-5980-0
eBook: 978-1-5381-9433- 1

Typeset by Deanta Global Publishing Services, Chennai, India

For product safety related questions contact productsafety@bloomsbury.com.

To find out more about our authors and books visit www.bloomsbury.com and
sign up for our newsletters.

Contents

Preface

Introduction

This section will introduce the authors as well as provide an outline of the book and what will be covered within it.

Chapter 1: History of Reproductive Rights in the United States

This chapter will present a timeline of reproductive rights in the United States, from the nation's first statutory abortion regulation in 1821 to the overturning of *Roe v. Wade* in 2022. This chapter is intended to provide readers with a background on protections and regulations around contraception and abortion in the United States as well as how and why abortion became the divisive political issue it is today. This chapter will also examine if and how mental health professionals have addressed reproductive rights with clients in the past.

Chapter 2: The Overturning of *Roe v. Wade*

This chapter will go into detail about the Supreme Court's decision, how it came to fruition, and reactions from various entities to the ruling. The efforts of post-Roe activists will be discussed, as will statements and actions taken by professional organizations. For example, a number of professional organizations, including the American Psychological Association, opposed the Supreme Court's decision, believing that the ruling will exacerbate the country's mental health crisis.

Chapter 3: Mental Health Impacts of the Ruling

Considerable research has found that people forced to carry unwanted pregnancies experience adverse financial, social, physical, and mental health effects (Herd et al., 2016; Londoño Tobón et al., 2023). The negative effects are more severe for survivors of domestic abuse/intimate partner violence or rape/incest and for people in marginalized groups, such as persons living in poverty or in medically underserved areas, people of color, and members of the LGBTQ+ community (Abrams, 2023; Ogbu-Nwobodo, 2022). This chapter will provide an overview of relevant research in this area and include personal stories from mental health professionals, clients, and others.

Chapter 4: Professional Ethics Codes

Ethical codes have been developed by various mental health associations for the purpose of setting professional standards for appropriate behavior, defining professional expectations, and preventing harm to clients. Mental health professionals have an obligation to be familiar with their professional code of ethics and its application to their professional services. This chapter will describe some of the most common ethical codes that mental health professionals follow, such as the American Psychological Association's (APA, 2017) *Ethical Principles of Psychologists and Code of Conduct*, the American Counseling Association's (ACA, 2014) *Code of Ethics*, and others.

Chapter 5: Relevant Laws

Following the reversal of *Roe v. Wade*, abortion has become illegal or heavily restricted in a number of US states, with additional restrictions likely to occur in other states. Mental health professionals may have many questions and concerns about facing possible criminal prosecution themselves for any role they may play in conversations about abortion with their clients. This chapter will provide information about current laws impacting clients and providers as well as answers to common questions and suggestions on how mental health providers can ensure they are practicing lawfully.

Chapter 6: Responsibilities and Implications for Mental Health Professionals

Now that the reader has gained a familiarity with the mental health impacts of the overturning of *Roe v. Wade* as well as with relevant professional ethics codes and laws, this chapter will examine the legal, ethical, and social justice responsibilities of and implications for mental health professionals. This chapter will describe implications for clinical practice, education/ supervision, research, and advocacy.

About the Authors

Jennifer Toof, PhD, LPC, NCC, is the owner/founder of Trauma Informed Counseling & Consulting, through which she provides trauma-informed mental health counseling services to children and adults and trauma/mental health consulting services to organizations. She holds a PhD in International Psychology from The Chicago School with a focus on trauma services. She has presented on a wide array of subjects at national and international professional conferences, including presenting on the topic of this book at the 2023 American Psychological Association conference in Washington, D.C., an endeavor that ultimately led to this book's publication. Dr. Toof sees clear parallels between counseling and advocacy, and, in both her personal and professional work, she advocates for the well-being of clients, counselors, the counseling profession, and society as a whole through various efforts, many of which involve political work/legislative advocacy.

Ami Crowley, EdD, NCC, ICADC, MCAP, BC-TMH, ACS, LMHC, is the co-owner and founder of Infinity Counseling Services, LLC, through which she provides both mental health and substance abuse services to a vast array of clients, as well as consulting services to organizations in the community. In addition, she is a full-time associate professor and Assistant Director of Clinical Training at The Chicago School in the Online Counselor Education Department, which focuses on trauma-informed care as well as teledelivery of services. Dr. Crowley has presented on a number of topics at the local, state, and national levels. Advocacy has always been a passion of Dr. Crowley's as she strongly believes in the responsibility that all professionals have to work toward improving care and access to services, serving underprivileged populations, and actively working toward the legislative change needed to meet the diverse needs of our populations.

About the Book

Mental health professionals are educated in and trained on how to help clients cope with stressful life experiences. However, when it comes to issues of reproductive rights, the political and highly divisive nature of the subject, along with fears of how to ethically and legally respond, can complicate the therapeutic process and leave professionals unsure of how to proceed (Rubin & Russo, 2004). To be competent mental health professionals, instructors, supervisors, researchers, and advocates, it is vital to understand the contemporary landscape of reproductive health issues that affects individuals, families, and communities (Grzanka & Frantell, 2017). The debate around abortion is often overtaken by political, ideological, and religious realms, but it is important to note that the subject is also a matter of physical and mental health and health care access. Issues of reproductive health are considered by many professionals to be central to mental health and to a social justice-focused counseling psychology (Grzanka & Frantell, 2017; Rubin & Russo, 2004).

In June 2022, the US Supreme Court overturned *Roe v. Wade*, the landmark piece of legislation which had previously protected the rights of Americans to seek abortions. Now, individual states are free to outright ban or severely limit Americans' rights to a procedure that had been legal since 1973. This ruling threw the country into a tailspin and put mental health professionals in the challenging position of wondering how they can best support clients impacted by the ruling while also abiding by pertinent laws and ethical codes.

This book seeks to help mental health professionals navigate their roles and responsibilities in a highly politically charged situation. Readers will learn about the history of reproductive rights in the United States, the landmark verdicts of *Roe v. Wade* and *Dobbs v. Jackson*, and the responses from the general public, professional organizations, and activists to the Dobbs verdict and the overturning of *Roe v. Wade*. This book will also help professionals understand the various ways the overturning of *Roe v. Wade* may impact the clients with whom they work, as considerable research has found that people forced to carry unwanted pregnancies experience adverse financial, social, physical, and mental health effects (Herd et al., 2016; Londoño Tobón et al., 2023). As discussed in this text, negative effects are more severe for people in marginalized groups, such as persons living in poverty, people of color, members of the LGBTQ+ community, and those in medically underserved areas (Abrams, 2023; Ogbu-Nwobodo, 2022).

Should mental health professionals set aside their personal thoughts and feelings about abortion to best serve their clients, and is this even possible? What do the ethical codes that mental health professionals abide by suggest for traversing this situation? This book encourages deep personal reflection while broadening professionals' understanding of the mental health effects of the ruling and providing insight into its ethical and social justice implications.

This book further describes some of the laws that may impact mental health professionals working with clients impacted by abortion regulations. The legislative situation changes rapidly, with new developments happening nearly every week. The information about laws in this text should not in any way be considered legal advice, and the authors strongly encourage mental health professionals to stay abreast of legal developments that may impact their work and to consult carefully with supervisors and attorneys when necessary.

References

Abrams, Z. (2023, June 1). Abortion bans cause outsized harm for people of color. *Monitor on Psychology.* https://www.apa.org/monitor/2023/06/abortion-bans-harm-people-of-color

Grzanka, P. R., & Frantell, K. A. (2017). Counseling psychology and reproductive justice: A call to action. *The Counseling Psychologist, 45*(3), 326–352. https://doi.org/10.1177/0011000017699871

Herd, P., Higgins, J., Sicinski, K., & Merkurieva, I. (2016). The implications of unintended pregnancies for mental health in later life. *American Journal of Public Health, 106*(3), 421–429. https://doi.org/10.2105/AJPH.2015.302973

Londoño Tobón, A., McNicholas, E., Clare, C. A., Ireland, L. D., Payne, J. L., Moore Simas, T. A., Scott, R. K., Becker, M., & Byatt, N. (2023). The end of Roe v. Wade: implications for women's mental health and care. *Frontiers in Psychiatry, 14*, 1087045–1087045. https://doi.org/10.3389/fpsyt.2023.1087045

Ogbu-Nwobodo, L., Shim, R. S., Vinson, S. Y., Fitelson, E. M., Biggs, M. A., McLemore, M. R., Thomas, M., Godzich, M., & Mangurian, C. (2022). Mental health implications of abortion restrictions for historically marginalized populations. *The New England Journal of Medicine, 387*(17), 1613–1617. https:// doi.org/10.1056/NEJMms2211124

Rubin, L., & Russo, N. F. (2004). Abortion and mental health: What therapists need to know. *Women & Therapy, 27*(3–4), 69–90. https://doi.org/10.1300/J015v27n03_06

History of Reproductive Rights in the United States

Jennifer Toof

Learning about the history of reproductive rights in the United States can help mental health professionals to be informed on the issue and engender critical thinking on how protections and regulations around contraception and abortion have historically impacted individuals, families, and communities. This chapter presents a basic timeline of reproductive rights in the United States, from the nation's first statutory abortion regulation in Connecticut in 1821 to the overturning of *Roe v. Wade* in 2022. Readers will learn how abortion became the divisive political issue it is today and how viewpoints on abortion have changed over time. Finally, this chapter provides readers with information on if and how mental health professionals have addressed reproductive rights with clients in the past.

Legal Timeline

Reproductive issues were largely private matters in early American history, so the exact number of abortions that occurred during this time is unknown (Mohr, 1978; Pew Research Center, 2008). Doctors and midwives performed abortions, guided by easily accessible information in medical guides and health books about drugs, potions, and techniques that could induce abortion (Kennedy, 2023; Mohr, 1978). Although they were technically illegal under English common law, the US government in the late 1700s and early 1800s took little interest in prosecuting cases of abortion that became public (Pew Research Center, 2008).

Most Americans did not consider abortion to be morally wrong as long as it was performed prior to a stage known as quickening (Mohr, 1978). Quickening was defined as the point at which fetal movement could be detected, which was generally considered to be around the fourth or fifth month of pregnancy (Kennedy, 2023; Mohr, 1978; Pew Research Center, 2008). The belief of most Americans at the time was that a fetus that could move was categorically different from one that could not, which was considered "an inanimate embryo" (Mohr, 1978, p. 23).

The first statutory abortion regulation in the United States was passed in Connecticut in 1821, and it made medicinal abortion illegal after the quickening stage (Kennedy, 2023). Arguably, the intent of the law was to protect the life of the pregnant woman as opposed to the life of the fetus. That is, the law only made one specific method of inducing an abortion illegal, that of administering a deadly poison or other noxious and destructive substance (Mohr, 1978). The reason this particular abortion method was named in the law was because of how unsafe the poisons and other substances were and how likely they were to cause the death of the pregnant individual (Mohr, 1978). Additionally, the law stated that it would be the person who provided the substances used to perform the abortion who would be charged with a crime, not the person receiving the abortion (Kennedy, 2023; Mohr, 1978). The punishment for those who were found to have provided abortion drugs was a life sentence (Kennedy, 2023).

In the twenty years following the 1821 Connecticut statute, nine additional states and one federal territory enacted similar legislation, making abortions explicit state offenses (Kennedy, 2023). In 1857, led by a man named Horatio Storer, the American Medical Association (AMA) campaigned to make abortion illegal in the entire country (Kennedy, 2023). Horatio Storer was an obstetrician often referred to as the father of American gynecology (Blakemore, 2019). Storer believed that women had both a social and a biological obligation to be wives and mothers and that abortion was therefore a disruption to how society should ideally function (Blakemore, 2019). He believed women who wanted abortions were mentally insane, and he did not want the medical profession associated with abortion (Blakemore, 2019). By 1860, three years after Storer and the AMA's campaigns began, more than twenty states had criminalized abortion (Kennedy, 2023). That same year, Connecticut law made the woman herself guilty of a felony if she attempted to have an abortion (Mohr, 1978).

On March 3, 1873, the US Congress passed the Comstock Act, making it a federal crime to sell or distribute contraception through the mail or across state lines (Kennedy, 2023). Drafted by Anthony Comstock, a devout Christian known for his "anti-vice" crusade against prostitution, pornography, and birth control, the statute termed birth control as "obscene" (Kennedy, 2023, para. 7). Twenty-four states enacted their own laws restricting access to contraception shortly after the passing of the Comstock Act (Kennedy, 2023). Between 1860 and 1880, over forty new anti-abortion statutes were enacted, most of which made abortion at any point in pregnancy a crime (Mohr, 1978). By the early 1900s, the majority of US states had outlawed abortion, with exceptions for when the pregnant woman's life or health was in danger (Pew Research Center, 2008). However, it was not always clear what health concerns would justify a legal abortion (Pew Research Center, 2008).

Despite the mounting anti-abortion laws in the United States, Americans did not stop getting abortions; rather, they simply went underground and found clandestine methods in which to end pregnancies (Blakemore, 2019). Although premarital sex was common, women in the late 1800s and early 1900s who had children outside of marriage were still considered fornicators, "fallen women," or even criminals (Blakemore, 2019, para. 16). Unmarried pregnant women were often cast out by their families and society, which was a highly problematic fate for women at the time, since they were discouraged from working and could not own property (Blakemore, 2019). Having an abortion was seen by some women as a way to escape such an outcome.

In spite of the increasing prohibitions on abortion and contraception in the United States, the early 1900s ushered forth a time of advocacy for greater political and sexual freedom for women (Pew Research Center, 2008). Margaret Sanger opened the country's first birth control clinic in Brooklyn, New York, in 1916, and the highly vocal women's suffrage movement gave women the right to vote in 1920 (Kennedy, 2023; Pew Research Center, 2008). Birth control options were becoming more favored, as people were opting for smaller families and as new notions of sexuality emphasized its pleasurable nature (Pew Research Center, 2008). In 1936, thanks in part to behind-the-scenes work by Sanger, a Court of Appeals ruled in favor of an amendment to the Comstock laws that would make it legal for doctors to distribute contraceptives across state lines (Kennedy, 2023).

The latter half of the 1900s led to increased medical developments for contraception, with Enovid, the nation's first oral contraceptive, gaining FDA approval in 1960 and the intrauterine device (IUD) gaining approval in 1968 (Kennedy, 2023). The 1960s and 1970s were also times of great legal changes with regard to abortion. In 1966, nine doctors in San Francisco were sued by the California State Board of Medical Examiners for performing abortions on women exposed to rubella, which was known to cause miscarriage, stillbirth, and severe birth defects (Kennedy, 2023). People across the country, including doctors and medical school deans, rallied in defense of the doctors, and the cases against them were dropped in 1970 (Kennedy, 2023). In 1967, Colorado was the first state in the union to loosen abortion restrictions, making it legal in cases where the woman's physical or mental health were at risk, in cases of incest or rape (including statutory rape), and in cases where the pregnancy was likely to result in birth defects (Kennedy, 2023). By 1970, eleven other states made similar changes to add exceptions to their laws, and four states (New York, Washington, Hawaii, and Alaska) completely decriminalized abortion during the early stages of pregnancy (Kennedy, 2023; Pew Research Center, 2008).

The landmark case of *Roe v. Wade* first began when a pregnant woman in Texas, using the pseudonym Jane Roe, challenged the constitutionality of the Texas laws that restricted abortion (Ball, 2010). The other name attached to the case, Wade, was that of the local district attorney in Texas (Ball, 2010). Roe wrote in her complaint to the federal district court in Dallas that her life was not threatened by her pregnancy but that she wanted an abortion performed by a doctor and could not afford to travel to another state, where abortion was legal, to receive one (Ball, 2010). Other women would later join Roe in her suit (Ball, 2010). Attorney for the plaintiffs Sarah Weddington believed that the case was a class action suit for all women who may one day want the option to have a legal abortion regardless of where they lived (Ball, 2010). The Dallas court ruled in favor of Roe, believing that Texas abortion laws were unconstitutionally vague (Ball, 2010). The case then went to the Supreme Court on appeal. Ultimately, on January 22, 1973, the US Supreme Court struck down the Texas law banning abortions and ruled 7–2 that the right to abortion was protected under the US Constitution's Fourteenth Amendment, which focuses on one's rights to privacy and liberty (Kennedy, 2023; Pew Research Center, 2008).

The Supreme Court decision specified that states could in no way limit access to abortions in the first trimester (labeled the first tier by Justice Harry Blackmun) and that states could only impose basic health safeguards during this time, such as requiring that qualified health practitioners perform the procedure (Kennedy, 2023; Pew Research Center, 2008). In the second trimester or second tier, which was determined to last from the end of the first trimester to the point of fetal viability, or between about twenty-four and twenty-eight weeks, the Court ruled that states could regulate abortions but only to protect the health of the mother (Kennedy, 2023; Pew Research Center, 2008). For example, state laws requiring doctors to receive informed consent from the mother before performing abortions would be constitutional as long as the intent was to protect the mother's health rather than to dissuade her from having an abortion (Pew Research Center, 2008). The final trimester, labeled the third tier by the Court, referred to the time at which the fetus could survive outside the womb, either naturally or through artificial means (Pew Research Center, 2008). In this period of pregnancy, the Court ruled that states could legally prohibit abortions as long as they remained legal in cases where the life or health of the mother was at risk (Pew Research Center, 2008).

Although *Roe v. Wade* was a win for abortion rights activists, there were successful efforts to restrict abortion in the years that followed the verdict, including on the federal level. The Hyde Amendment, named after its original sponsor, Representative Henry J. Hyde, an outspoken opponent of abortion, was first passed in 1976 and barred federal funding (i.e., Medicaid coverage) for abortions except in cases where the woman's life was in danger if she did not have one (Congressional Research Services, 2022; North, 2019). The Hyde Amendment has been renewed annually since its introduction, with newer versions allowing exceptions for abortions to pregnancies resulting from rape or incest (Congressional Research Services, 2022).

The three-tier framework created through Roe was partly dismantled and modified in the 1992 case of *Planned Parenthood of Southeastern Pennsylvania v. Casey* (Kennedy, 2023). While the Supreme Court upheld their previous ruling affirming abortion rights, this verdict gave more authority to states (Kennedy, 2023; Pew Research Center, 2008). States could now regulate abortion at any point before fetal viability and for reasons other than protecting the health of the mother (Kennedy, 2023; Pew Research Center, 2008). Since then, states have enacted various pieces of legislation aimed at regulating abortions, with one of the most controversial recent bills being SB 8, the Texas Heartbeat Act of 2021 (Kennedy, 2023). The Texas Heartbeat Act effectively banned abortions after an embryo's heartbeat can be detected, at six weeks, with no exceptions for rape or incest. The act also allows private citizens the ability to sue any person who "aids or abets" an abortion after a heartbeat is detected (Kennedy, 2023).

On June 24, 2022, the US Supreme Court decided the case of *Dobbs v. Jackson Women's Health Organizatio*n, ruling 6–3 to overturn *Roe v. Wade* (Kennedy, 2023). This ruling meant that people no longer had a constitutional right to an abortion and that abortion laws were now left entirely up to each state (Kennedy, 2023). The following chapter will go into more detail on the overturning of *Roe v. Wade* and responses to the verdict. Since the Dobbs decision, nearly two dozen US states have restricted abortion to a level that would not have been legal under Roe, including fourteen states with near-total bans on abortion (John, 2024; Mane et al., 2022). Additionally, in May 2024, Louisiana passed a law labeling abortion pills as controlled substances, making it a felony to possess the drugs without a prescription (John, 2024). As of the time of this writing, state courts in over a dozen states are hearing challenges to abortion bans and other restrictions (John, 2024).

Politicization of Abortion

At the time of the *Roe v. Wade* verdict in 1973, abortion was not the highly partisan issue it is today. Neither Democrats nor Republicans viewed abortion as a defining issue of their platform, and it was not at all uncommon to find

Democratic officials who opposed the procedure and Republican officials who supported it (Sullivan, 2022). For example, newly elected senator Joe Biden said at the time of the verdict that the Supreme Court "went too far" in codifying abortion rights into law, while First Lady Betty Ford (wife of Republican then-president Gerald Ford) lauded it as "a great, great decision" (Sullivan, 2022). Voters also did not see the issue along partisan lines at that time. A 1977 General Social Survey opinion found that 39 percent of Republicans said abortion should be allowed for any reason, compared to just 35 percent of Democrats (Sullivan, 2022).

It was activists who began pushing politicians and trying to influence the public either for or against abortion regulations (North, 2019; Sullivan, 2022). For example, religious/evangelical groups portrayed abortion as a threat to the family structure, while women's rights activists pushed leaders to support abortion rights and one's liberty to choose (Sullivan, 2022). The Republican party, eager to be seen as pro-family, began to mobilize socially conservative voters and forged coalitions with evangelical groups around opposition to abortion (North, 2019). Between 1976 and 1980, the Christian right, a largely Southern conservative faction, began to emerge as an influential voting bloc, and Ronald Reagan aligned himself with this group (Bartho, 2024). In the 1984 Presidential election, incumbent Reagan defeated pro-choice Democrat Walter Mondale by a wide margin. Voters that year were more divided over abortion than they were in 1980 (Granberg, 1987). That is, in 1980, Reagan voters and Carter voters did not differ significantly in their attitudes toward abortion, but, in 1984, Reagan voters were significantly more likely to be opposed to abortion than Mondale voters (Granberg, 1987). That said, it was still only a small minority of voters who considered abortion to be a major national issue, and there was no consensus regarding abortion among political parties as a whole (Granberg, 1987).

In another example of party affiliation and abortion views in the late nineteenth century being very different than they are today, Bob Casey Sr., namesake of the previously mentioned case of *Planned Parenthood v. Casey*, was the Democratic governor of Pennsylvania when his case went to the Supreme Court. A Catholic, Casey Sr. was staunchly pro-life, and, in a 1987 speech, he called abortion "the ultimate violence" (Kengor, 2022). Casey Sr.

easily won reelection as the Democratic candidate for governor in 1990 by a margin of 35.29 percent, winning sixty-six of Pennsylvania's sixty-seven counties (Kennedy, 2006). His Republican opponent, Barbara Hafer, was vocally pro-choice (Kennedy, 2006). Notably, Hafer became a registered Democrat in 2003 and sought the Democratic nomination for Congress in 2010 (Gibson, 2012).

Over time, partisan affiliations came to supplant the role of religion in predicting abortion support. Political candidates increasingly found it necessary to align with a side on the abortion debate, with the Republican party leaning more toward opposing abortion rights and the Democratic party leaning more toward supporting abortion rights. Public opinion started to change as well, with a 1991 survey finding that 45 percent of Democrats and 41 percent of Republicans said they supported abortion for any reason, and, by 2000, only 31 percent of Republicans supported abortion for any reason, while Democratic support remained steady at 45 percent (Sullivan, 2022).

In 2024, per the Pew Research Center, 63 percent of Americans said they believe abortion should be legal in all or most cases, while 36 percent said they believe it should be illegal in all or most cases. The current party division is significant: 85 percent of Democrats and Independents who lean toward the Democratic party said that abortion should be legal in all or most cases compared to 41 percent of Republicans and Independents who lean toward the Republican party with the same view (Pew Research Center, 2024); 71 percent of Republicans who consider themselves conservative said that abortion should be illegal in all or most cases, while just 31 percent of Republicans who consider themselves moderate or liberal believe it should be illegal in all or most cases (Pew Research Center, 2024). Comparatively, 96 percent of Democrats who consider themselves liberal and 76 percent of Democrats who consider themselves moderate or conservative said they support legal abortion in all or most cases (Pew Research Center, 2024).

With regard to religion, 73 percent of white evangelical Protestants said abortion should be illegal in all or most cases (Pew Research Center, 2024). Also, 86 percent of Americans who labeled themselves as religiously unaffiliated said abortion should be legal in all or most cases, as did 71 percent of Black Protestants, 64 percent of white non-evangelical Protestants, and

59 percent of Catholics (Pew Research Center, 2024). Polling found that there is equal support for legal abortion among men and women, with 61 percent of men and 64 percent of women saying abortion should be legal in all or most cases (Pew Research Center, 2024). Furthermore, 76 percent of Asian adults, 73 percent of Black adults, 60 percent of white adults, and 59 percent of Hispanic adults in the United States support legal abortion for all or most cases (Pew Research Center, 2024). Also, 76 percent of Americans under the age of thirty said abortion should be legal in all or most cases, as did 61 percent of Americans in their thirties and forties, 57 percent of Americans in their fifties and early sixties, and 59 percent of Americans aged sixty-five or older (Pew Research Center, 2024). Finally, with regard to education, 68 percent of college graduates said abortion should be legal in all or most cases, as did 64 percent of those with some college education and 56 percent of those with a high school degree or less education (Pew Research Center, 2024).

Mental Health Professionals Addressing Reproductive Rights with Clients

It is important to distinguish between mental health professionals working with clients who are having or who have had abortions and "abortion counselors," who are not always mental health professionals. Millner and Hanks (2002, p. 58) wrote that "abortion counselors" generally work directly in family planning or abortion clinics and that their main function is to ensure patients coming in for abortions are adequately informed of and prepared for the procedure. Abortion counseling has generally involved three separate functions: obtaining informed consent, which includes ruling out coercion; patient education, which involves explaining the technical aspects of the procedure and possible complications; and counseling, which involves addressing the patient's feelings about the procedure (Joffe, 2013).

Abortion counseling was common in the first freestanding abortion clinics established in New York City, New York, and Washington, D.C. (Joffe, 2013). The clinic founders, who were mainly physicians, decided to include abortion counseling because they noticed a dearth of knowledge surrounding abortion

(Joffe, 2013). The belief that people who are considering abortion require some sort of counseling was held by many physicians and medical groups in the late 1960s and early 1970s. The Group for the Advancement of Psychiatry (1970, as cited in Asher, 1972) wrote:

> As psychiatrists we would particularly emphasize the importance of the physician's exploring with the pregnant woman the basis of her motivation so as to clarify impulsive, or self-destructive elements in the decision to abort. The various medical judgments pertinent to abortion may, when warranted, be arrived at with the help of consultation. We do not believe that psychiatric consultation should necessarily be routine. (p. 686)

The American Public Health Association (1970, as cited in Asher, 1972) wrote the following in its Recommended Standards for Abortion Services:

> Counseling is an integral part of abortion services. The manner in which referral and counseling are carried out plays a major role in determining whether the abortion patient is treated in a safe, humane, and dignified manner, and protected against exploitation. (p. 686)

Dr. John Asher, former chief resident in the Department of Psychiatry at Stanford University, wrote in a 1971 article that abortion counseling must be entered into freely and that the "single most important function of the counselor is to help the woman weigh the alternatives and arrive at her own decision" (p. 687). Historically, informed consent has been a legal requirement before someone could have an abortion performed. In addition to ensuring the person is not being coerced into receiving the procedure, informed consent also involves patients being provided adequate and appropriate information. Unfortunately, however, those providing abortion counseling have not always kept their own biases out of their work and have not always given factual information, and reproductive rights advocates argue that some of the legal requirements of abortion counseling serve to discourage people from getting the procedure (Guttmacher Institute, 2024; Temple University Center for Public Health Law Research, 2022).

At the time of writing, thirty-three states require that patients receive abortion counseling from a physician or other qualified individual before they can have an abortion (Guttmacher Institute, 2024; Temple University

Center for Public Health Law Research, 2022). Twenty-eight of these states also require patients to wait a specified amount of time, usually twenty-four hours, between counseling and the abortion procedure, thereby necessitating two separate trips to the facility (Guttmacher Institute, 2024). Nearly all the states that require this type of counseling include information about the abortion procedure and fetal development (Guttmacher Institute, 2024). With regard to information provided in abortion counseling that reproductive rights advocates say is misleading and may discourage people from getting an abortion, fourteen states include information on the ability of a fetus to feel pain, five states require that patients be told that personhood begins at conception, and eight of the twenty-two states that include information on possible psychological responses to abortion focus on negative emotional effects (Guttmacher Institute, 2024; Temple University Center for Public Health Law Research, 2022). It is legally required in eight US states that patients receive the inaccurate information that a medication abortion can be stopped after the patient takes the first dose of pills (Guttmacher Institute, 2024). Additionally, five of the eight states that include information on breast cancer inaccurately assert a link between abortion and an increased risk of breast cancer, and three states inaccurately portray the risk of abortion on future fertility (Guttmacher Institute, 2024).

Abortion counseling, as described, is obviously very different from the type of counseling generally provided by licensed mental health professionals. Before the overturning of *Roe v. Wade*, there was little mention in professional literature of how mental health professionals handled legal and ethical issues related to reproductive rights with clients. Published recommendations for such practitioners in dealing specifically with the issue have been limited in both number and scope (Millner & Hanks, 2002). However, a 2002 article by Millner and Hanks noted that the "divergent ethical and legal issues involving intense value conflicts" about abortion could impact counselors as well as clients (p. 1). They wrote that a legal concern relevant to counselors addressing abortion in sessions with clients is tort law, involving negligence, and how counselors could be held legally responsible for negligence by not exercising reasonable care. For example, Millner and Hanks (2002) wrote that counselors could be held liable for negligence if they withheld pertinent information or provided false information about abortion, did not refer the client, or made an inadequate client referral, such as by referring the client to a facility that supports the counselor's, rather than the client's, values surrounding abortion.

In the absence of other laws related to discussing reproductive rights with clients, ethical issues have been the main concern for mental health professionals working with clients talking about abortion. As will be discussed thoroughly in other chapters of this book, mental health professionals rely on ethical standards, such as the American Counseling Association *Code of Ethics and Standards of Practice*, to guide their work. Although every version of the American Counseling Association's ethical code, starting from its original 1961 version, has noted that the counselor has a primary obligation to respect the integrity and promote the welfare of the person with whom they are working, it was not until the 1995 version that specific reference was made to counselors being aware of their own values, attitudes, and personal beliefs (American Counseling Association, 1995). Perhaps more importantly when considering divisive issues such as abortion, the 1995 version of the ethical code also stipulated that counselors avoid imposing their own values on clients (American Counseling Association, 1995). However, even before the publishing of the ethical code, there were professional recommendations for counselors to possess awareness of if and how personal beliefs, including on issues such as abortion, may compromise the counseling relationship. For example, Armsworth noted in 1991 that, given the complexity and emotionally charged nature of abortion, counselors should clarify their own views on the issue before working with clients faced with abortion-related decisions. Corey et al. (1993) similarly asserted not only the importance of counselors clarifying their own views but also of recognizing if and how one's values may interfere with the objectivity needed to be effective with clients.

Such recommendations, and ethical guidelines, have remained for counseling professionals in the years to follow. A subsequent chapter of this book discusses in greater detail how research has found that most people who have an abortion do not experience mental health difficulties afterward. Thus, more recent articles that exist on working with clients who are considering an abortion or who have had an abortion often focus on how to support the individual client's needs and feelings about the procedure. For example, Bray

(2018) wrote that, despite the counselors' personal views, counselors should focus on allowing the client a safe and nonjudgmental space to share.

Conclusion

This chapter has provided a timeline revealing how legal and societal changes have influenced the perception and political landscape of abortion in the United States. By examining the history of reproductive rights, mental health professionals are better positioned to understand the complexities of this issue and its effects on individuals and communities. Considering the evolving political and social climate, possessing this knowledge can not only foster critical thinking but also enhance one's ability to engage with clients on reproductive rights.

Discussion Questions

1) How have the perceptions of reproductive rights evolved from the 19th century to the present day? What significant historical events may have influenced these changes?
2) In what ways has religion influenced the dialogue and legislation surrounding reproductive rights? How do differing religious beliefs impact individuals' perspectives on issues like abortion and contraception?
3) How does the history of reproductive rights in the United States compare to that of other countries? What can be learned from these comparisons regarding the effectiveness of various policies and approaches?

References

American Counseling Association. (1995). *1995 ACA code of ethics & standards of practice* . https://www.counseling.org/docs/default-source/ethics/archived-code-of -ethics/code-of-ethics-1995.pdf?sfvrsn=a92f3a61_2

Armsworth, M. W. (1991). Psychological response to abortion. *Journal of Counseling & Development, 69*, 377–379.

Asher, J. D. (1972). Abortion counseling. *American Journal of Public Health (1971), 62*(5), 686–688. https://doi.org/10.2105/AJPH.62.5.686

Ball, M. J. (2010). *The abortion attitudes of counselor, social worker, and nursing trainees* -(Dissertations), p. 499. https://scholarworks.wmich.edu/dissertations/499

Bartho, J. (2024, April 12). How Ronald Reagan helped abortion take over the Republican agenda. *Time.* https://time.com/6966056/republican-abortion-arizona -reagan/

Blakemore, E. (2019, May 15). The criminalization of abortion as a business tactic. *History.* https://www.history.com/news/the-criminalization-of-abortion-began-as -a-business-tactic

Bray, B. (2018, April 03). When post-abortion emotions need unpacking. *Counseling Today.* https://ctarchive.counseling.org/2018/04/when-post-abortion-emotions -need-unpacking/

Congressional Research Service. (2022). *The Hyde Amendment: An overview.* https:// crsreports.congress.gov/product/pdf/IF/IF12167

Corey, G., Corey, M. S., & Callanan, P. (1993). *Issues and ethics in the helping professions.* Brooke/Cole.

Gibson, K. (2012, November 04). Hafer crosses party lines (again), endorses Maher. *Politics PA.* https://www.politicspa.com/hafer-crosses-party-lines-again-endorses -maher/43885/

Granberg, D. (1987). The abortion issue in the 1984 elections. *Family Planning Perspectives, 19*(2), 59–62.

Guttmacher Institute. (2024). *Counseling and waiting periods for abortion.* https:// www.guttmacher.org/state-policy/explore/counseling-and-waiting-periods -abortion

John, A. (2024, June 21). The political landscape remains unsettled two years post-Roe. *CNN.* https://www.cnn.com/2024/06/21/politics/state-abortion-laws-post -roe/index.html

Joffe, C. (2013). The politicization of abortion and the evolution of abortion counseling. *American Journal of Public Health, 103*(1), 57–65. https://doi.org/10.2105/AJPH.2012.301063

Kengor, P. (2022, November 09). Pennsylvania: A tale of 2 Caseys and the death of a pro-life Catholic state. *EWTN.* https://ewtn.co.uk/pennsylvania-a-tale-of-2-caseys-and-the-death-of-a-pro-life-catholic-state/

Kennedy, J. J. (2006). *Pennsylvania elections: Statewide contests from 1950–2004.* University Press of America.

Kennedy, L. (2023, July 13). Reproductive rights in the US: Timeline. *History.* https://www.history.com/news/reproductive-rights-timeline

Mane, H., Yue, X., Yu, W., Doig, A. C., Wei, H., Delcid, N., Harris, A. G., Nguyen, T. T., & Nguyen, Q. C. (2022). Examination of the public's reaction on Twitter to the over-turning of Roe v Wade and abortion bans. *Healthcare (Basel, Switzerland), 10*(12), 2390. https://doi.org/10.3390/healthcare10122390

Millner, V. S., & Hanks, R. B. (2002). Induced abortion: An ethical conundrum for counselors. *Journal of Counseling & Development, 80,* 57–63. https://doi-org.tcsedsystem.idm.oclc.org/10.1002/j.1556-6678.2002.tb00166.x

Mohr, J. C. (1978). *Abortion in America: The origins and evolution of national policy.* Oxford University Press.

North, A. (2019, April 10). How abortion became a partisan issue in America. *Vox.* https://www.vox.com/2019/4/10/18295513/abortion-2020-roe-joe-biden-democrats-republicans

Pew Research Center. (2008, January 17). *From Roe to Stenberg: A history of key abortion rulings by the supreme court.* https://www.pewresearch.org/religion/2008/01/17/from-roe-to-stenberg-a-history-of-key-abortion-rulings-by-the-supreme-court/

Pew Research Center. (2024, May 13). *Public opinion on abortion.* https://www.pewresearch.org/religion/fact-sheet/public-opinion-on-abortion/

Sullivan, A. (2022, June 24). Explainer: How abortion became a divisive issue in U.S. politics. *Reuters.* https://www.reuters.com/world/us/how-abortion-became-divisive-issue-us-politics-2022-06-24/

Temple University Center for Public Health Law Research. (2022). *Pre-abortion requirements.* www.LawAtlas.org/datasets/abortion-waiting-period-requirements

The Overturning of *Roe v. Wade*

Jennifer Toof

With contributions from Mandy McGuire Schwartz & Alex Luckanish

The proceeding chapter goes into further detail about the US Supreme Court's decision to overturn *Roe v. Wade*, including how the verdict came to fruition and responses to the ruling from political leaders, the general public, and professional organizations. This chapter also discusses the actions of people on both sides of the abortion debate following the verdict.

Dobbs v. Jackson

The case of *Dobbs v. Jackson Women's Health Organization*, shortened to *Dobbs v. Jackson*, was filed in March of 2018 by the Center for Reproductive Rights (n.d.) on behalf of Jackson Women's Health Organization. Jackson Women's Health Organization was the last remaining abortion clinic in Mississippi at the time, and the organization sought to block Mississippi's ban on abortion after fifteen weeks of pregnancy, claiming it was unconstitutional (Center for Reproductive Rights, n.d.). The case was filed just hours after then-governor of Mississippi Phil Bryant signed the Gestational Age Act into law on March 19, 2018, which banned most abortions after fifteen weeks of pregnancy, with exceptions for medical emergencies and fetal abnormalities (Center for Reproductive Rights, n.d.; National Constitution Center, 2024). A federal district court granted emergency relief the following day, which blocked enforcement of the abortion ban, and, in November of 2018, the federal district court struck down the law, agreeing with Jackson Women's Health

Organization and concluding that "[t]he State chose to pass a law it knew was unconstitutional to endorse a decades long campaign, fueled by national interest groups, to ask the Supreme Court to overturn Roe v. Wade" (Center for Reproductive Rights, n.d.).

The US Court of Appeals for the Fifth Circuit unanimously affirmed the district court's decision in December 2019, with Judge Patrick Higginbotham writing that "in an unbroken line dating to Roe v. Wade, the Supreme Court's abortion cases have established (and affirmed and reaffirmed) a woman's right to choose an abortion before viability" (Center for Reproductive Rights, n.d.). The state of Mississippi filed a petition asking the US Supreme Court to review the fifteen-week abortion ban on June 15, 2020, and the Court agreed to consider the question as to whether all pre-viability prohibitions on abortion are unconstitutional (Center for Reproductive Rights, n.d.). This marked the first time the Supreme Court considered a pre-viability abortion ban since *Roe v. Wade* (Center for Reproductive Rights, n.d.).

On May 3, 2022, Supreme Court Justice Samuel Alito's draft opinion in the *Dobbs v. Jackson Women's Health Organization* case was leaked, provoking strong public opinion (Mane et al., 2022). On June 24, 2022, the Supreme Court decided the *Dobbs v. Jackson* case, ruling 6–3, that the Mississippi law banning abortions after fifteen weeks, was constitutional (Center for Reproductive Rights, n.d.). The *Dobbs v. Jackson* verdict overruled both *Roe v. Wade* and *Planned Parenthood v. Casey*, and it meant that there was no longer any constitutional restriction on legislation banning abortion (Mane et al., 2022; National Constitution Center, 2024).

Opinions of the Supreme Court Justices involved in the decision are archived in the National Constitution Center (2024). Conservative Justice Samuel Alito wrote the majority opinion for the court, saying in part:

> We hold that Roe and Casey must be overruled. The Constitution makes no reference to abortion, and no such right is implicitly protected by any constitutional provision, including the one on which the defenders of Roe and Casey now chiefly rely—the Due Process Clause of the Fourteenth Amendment. That provision has been held to guarantee some rights that are not mentioned in the Constitution, but any such right must be "deeply

rooted in this Nation's history and tradition" and "implicit in the concept of ordered liberty."

The right to abortion does not fall within this category. (National Constitution Center, 2024)

Justice Brett Kanavaugh, who was appointed to the Supreme Court by Donald Trump in 2018, agreed, stating:

The issue before this Court . . . is not the policy or morality of abortion. The issue before the Court is what the Constitution says about abortion. The Constitution does not take sides on the issue of abortion. . . . On the question of abortion, the Constitution is . . . neither pro-life nor pro-choice. The Constitution is neutral and leaves the issue for the people and their elected representatives to resolve through the democratic process in the States or Congress. (National Constitution Center, 2024)

In a joint dissent, Justices Stephen Breyer, Elena Kagan, and Sonia Sotomayor issued the following minority opinion, disagreeing with the majority's interpretation of the Constitution, decrying the verdict, and calling it a curtailment of women's rights:

For half a century, Roe v. Wade and Planned Parenthood of Southeastern Pa. v. Casey have protected the liberty and equality of women. Roe held, and Casey reaffirmed, that the Constitution safeguards a woman's right to decide for herself whether to bear a child. Roe held, and Casey reaffirmed, that in the first stages of pregnancy, the government could not make that choice for women. The government could not control a woman's body or the course of a woman's life: It could not determine what the woman's future would be. Respecting a woman as an autonomous being, and granting her full equality, meant giving her substantial choice over this most personal and most consequential of all life decisions.

The Court struck a balance, as it often does when values and goals compete. It held that the State could prohibit abortions until after fetal viability, so long as the ban contained exceptions to safeguard a woman's life or health. It held that even before viability, the State could regulate the abortion procedure in multiple and meaningful ways. But until the viability line was crossed, the Court held, a State could not impose a "substantial obstacle" on a woman's "right to elect the procedure" as she (not the government) thought proper, in light of all the circumstances and complexities of her own life.

Today, the Court discards that balance. It says that from the very moment of fertilization, a woman has no rights to speak of. . . .

[O]ne result of today's decision is certain: the curtailment of women's rights, and of their status as free and equal citizens. Yesterday, the Constitution guaranteed that a woman confronted with an unplanned pregnancy could (within reasonable limits) make her own decision about whether to bear a child, with all the life-transforming consequences that act involves. And in thus safeguarding each woman's reproductive freedom, the Constitution also protected "[t]he ability of women to participate equally in [this Nation's] economic and social life." . . . But no longer. As of today, this Court holds, a State can always force a woman to give birth, prohibiting even the earliest abortions. A State can thus transform what, when freely undertaken, is a wonder into what, when forced, may be a nightmare. Some women, especially women of means, will find ways around the State's assertion of power. Others—those without money or childcare or the ability to take time off from work—will not be so fortunate. Maybe they will try an unsafe method of abortion, and come to physical harm, or even die. Maybe they will undergo pregnancy and have a child, but at significant personal or familial cost. At the least, they will incur the cost of losing control of their lives. The Constitution will, today's majority holds, provide no shield, despite its guarantees of liberty and equality for all.

And no one should be confident that this majority is done with its work. The right Roe and Casey recognized does not stand alone. To the contrary, the Court has linked it for decades to other settled freedoms involving bodily integrity, familial relationships, and procreation. Most obviously, the right to terminate a pregnancy arose straight out of the right to purchase and use contraception. . . . In turn, those rights led, more recently, to rights of same-sex intimacy and marriage. . . . They are all part of the same constitutional fabric, protecting autonomous decision making over the most personal of life decisions . . .

The majority has no good reason for the upheaval in law and society it sets off. Roe and Casey have been the law of the land for decades, shaping women's expectations of their choices when an unplanned pregnancy occurs. Women have relied on the availability of abortion both in structuring their relationships and in planning their lives. The legal framework Roe and

Casey developed to balance the competing interests in this sphere has proved workable in courts across the country. No recent developments, in either law or fact, have eroded or cast doubt on those precedents. Nothing, in short, has changed . . .

The Court reverses course today for one reason and one reason only: because the composition of this Court has changed. Stare decisis, this Court has often said, contributes to the actual and perceived integrity of the judicial process by ensuring that decisions are founded in the law rather than in the proclivities of individuals. Today, the proclivities of individuals rule. The Court departs from its obligation to faithfully and impartially apply the law. We dissent . . .

The majority would allow States to ban abortion from conception onward because it does not think forced childbirth at all implicates a woman's rights to equality and freedom. Today's Court, that is, does not think there is anything of constitutional significance attached to a woman's control of her body and the path of her life. Roe and Casey thought that one-sided view misguided. In some sense, that is the difference in a nutshell between our precedents and the majority opinion. The constitutional regime we have lived in for the last 50 years recognized competing interests, and sought a balance between them. The constitutional regime we enter today erases the woman's interest and recognizes only the State's (or the Federal Government's).

The majority makes this change based on a single question: Did the reproductive right recognized in Roe and Casey exist in "1868, the year when the Fourteenth Amendment was ratified?" . . . The majority says (and with this much we agree) that the answer to this question is no: In 1868, there was no nationwide right to end a pregnancy, and no thought that the Fourteenth Amendment provided one.

Of course, the majority opinion refers as well to some later and earlier history. On the one side of 1868, it goes back as far as the 13th (the 13th!) century. . . . But that turns out to be wheel-spinning. First, it is not clear what relevance such early history should have, even to the majority. . . . If the early history obviously supported abortion rights, the majority would no doubt say that only the views of the Fourteenth Amendment's ratifiers are germane. . . . Second—and embarrassingly for the majority—early law in fact does provide some support for abortion rights. Common-law authorities did not treat abortion as a crime before "quickening"—the point when the fetus moved in the womb. And early American law followed the common-law rule. So the criminal law of that early time might be taken as roughly consonant with Roe's and Casey's different treatment of early and late abortions. Better, then, to move forward in time. On the other side of 1868, the majority occasionally notes that many States barred abortion up to the time of Roe. That is convenient for the majority, but it is window dressing. . . . Had the pre-Roe liberalization of abortion laws occurred more quickly and more widely in the 20th century, the majority would say (once again) that only the ratifiers' views are germane.

The majority's core legal postulate, then, is that we in the 21st century must read the Fourteenth Amendment just as its ratifiers did. And that is indeed what the majority emphasizes over and over again. . . . If the ratifiers did not understand something as central to freedom, then neither can we. Or said more particularly: If those people did not understand reproductive rights as part of the guarantee of liberty conferred in the Fourteenth Amendment, then those rights do not exist.

As an initial matter, note a mistake in the just preceding sentence. We referred to the "people" who ratified the Fourteenth Amendment: What rights did those "people" have in their heads at the time? But, of course, "people" did not ratify the Fourteenth Amendment. Men did. So it is perhaps not so surprising that the ratifiers were not perfectly attuned to the importance of reproductive rights for women's liberty, or for their capacity to participate as equal members of our Nation. Indeed, the ratifiers—both in 1868 and when the original Constitution was approved in 1788—did not understand women as full members of the community embraced by the phrase "We the People." In 1868, the first wave of American feminists were explicitly told—of course by men—that it was not their time to seek constitutional protections. (Women would not get even the vote for another half-century.) . . . Those responsible for the original Constitution, including the Fourteenth Amendment, did not perceive women as equals, and did not recognize women's rights. When the majority says that we must read our foundational charter as viewed at the time of ratification (except that we may also check it against the Dark Ages), it consigns women to second-class citizenship . . .

So how is it that, as Casey said, our Constitution, read now, grants rights to women, though it did not in 1868? How is it that our Constitution subjects discrimination against them to heightened scrutiny? How is it that our Constitution, through the Fourteenth Amendment's liberty clause, guarantees access to contraception (also not legally protected in 1868) so that women can decide for themselves whether and when to bear a child? How is it that until today, that same constitutional clause protected a woman's right, in the event contraception failed, to end a pregnancy in its earlier stages?

The answer is that this Court has rejected the majority's pinched view of how to read our Constitution. . . . [I]n the words of the great Chief Justice John Marshall, our Constitution is "intended to endure for ages to come," and must adapt itself to a future "seen dimly," if at all. . . . That is indeed why our Constitution is written as it is. The Framers (both in 1788 and 1868) understood that the world changes. So they did not define rights by reference to the specific practices existing at the time. Instead, the Framers defined rights in general terms, to permit future evolution in their scope and meaning. And over the course of our history, this Court has taken up the Framers' invitation. It has kept true to the Framers' principles by applying them in new ways, responsive to new societal understandings and conditions . . .

Nowhere has that approach been more prevalent than in construing the majestic but open-ended words of the Fourteenth Amendment— the guarantees of "liberty" and "equality" for all. And nowhere has that approach produced prouder moments, for this country and the Court. Consider an example Obergefell used a few years ago. The Court there confronted a claim . . . that the Fourteenth Amendment "must be defined in a most circumscribed manner, with central reference to specific historical practices"—exactly the view today's majority follows. . . . And the Court specifically rejected that view. In doing so, the Court reflected on what the proposed, historically circumscribed approach would have meant of interracial marriage. The Fourteenth Amendment's ratifiers did not think it gave black and white people a right to marry each other. To the contrary, contemporaneous practice deemed that act quite as unprotected as abortion. Yet the Court in Loving v. Virginia read the Fourteenth Amendment to embrace the Lovings' union. If, Obergefell explained, "rights were defined by who exercised them in the past, then received practices could serve as their own continued justification"—even when they conflict with "liberty" and "equality" as later and more broadly understood. The Constitution does not freeze for all time the original view of what those rights guarantee, or how they apply.

That does not mean anything goes. The majority wishes people to think there are but two alternatives: (1) accept the original applications of the Fourteenth Amendment and no others, or (2) surrender to judges' "own ardent views," ungrounded in law, about the liberty that Americans should enjoy. . . . [A]pplications of liberty and equality can evolve while remaining grounded in constitutional principles, constitutional history, and constitutional precedents. The second Justice Harlan discussed how to strike the right balance when he explained why he would have invalidated a State's ban on contraceptive use. Judges, he said, are not 'free to roam where unguided speculation might take them. . . . Yet they also must recognize that the constitutional 'tradition' of this country is not captured whole at a single moment. Rather, its meaning gains content from the long sweep of our history and from successive judicial precedents—each looking to the last and each seeking to apply the Constitution's most fundamental commitments to new conditions. That is why Americans . . . have a right to marry across racial lines. And it is why, to go back to Justice Harlan's case, Americans have a right to use contraceptives so they can choose for themselves whether to have children. . . .

Faced with all these connections between Roe/Casey and judicial decisions recognizing other constitutional rights, the majority tells everyone not to worry. It can (so it says) neatly extract the right to choose from the constitutional edifice without affecting any associated rights. (Think of someone telling you that the Jenga tower simply will not collapse.). . . .

According to the majority, no liberty interest is present [in the context of abortion]—because (and only because) the law offered no protection to the woman's choice in the 19th century. But here is the rub. The law also did not then (and would not for ages) protect a wealth of other things. It did not protect the rights recognized in Lawrence and Obergefell to same-sex intimacy and marriage. It did not protect the right recognized in Loving to marry across racial lines. It did not protect the right recognized in Griswold to contraceptive use. For that matter, it did not protect the right . . . not to be sterilized without consent. So if the majority is right in its legal analysis, all those decisions were wrong, and all those matters properly belong to the States too—whatever the particular state interests involved. And if that is true, it is impossible to understand (as a matter of logic and principle) how the majority can say that its opinion today does not threaten—does not even "undermine"—any number of other constitutional rights.

Nor does it even help just to take the majority at its word. Assume the majority is sincere in saying, for whatever reason, that it will go so far and no further. Scout's honor. Still, the future significance of today's opinion will be decided in the future. And law often has a way of evolving without regard to original intentions—a way of actually following where logic leads, rather than tolerating hard-to-explain lines.

By overruling Roe, Casey, and more than 20 cases reaffirming or applying the constitutional right to abortion, the majority abandons stare decisis, a principle central to the rule of law. [In previous cases overturning precedent,] the Court found, for example, (1) a change in legal doctrine that undermined or made obsolete the earlier decision; (2) a factual change that had the same effect; or (3) an absence of reliance because the earlier decision was less than a decade old. . . . None of those factors apply here: Nothing—and in particular, no significant legal or factual change—supports overturning a half-century of settled law giving women control over their reproductive lives.

[The Court's decision] makes radical change too easy and too fast, based on nothing more than the new views of new judges. The majority has overruled Roe and Casey for one and only one reason: because it has always despised them, and now it has the votes to discard them. The majority thereby substitutes a rule by judges for the rule of law.

This Court will surely face critical question about how [its new approach] applies. Must a state law allow abortions when necessary to protect a woman's life and health? And if so, exactly when? How much risk to a woman's life can a State force her to incur, before the Fourteenth Amendment's protection of life kicks in? Suppose a patient with pulmonary hypertension has a 30-to-50 percent risk of dying with ongoing pregnancy; is that enough? And short of death, how much illness or injury can the State require her to accept, consistent with the Amendment's protection of liberty and equality? Further, the Court may face questions about the application of abortion regulations to medical care most people view as quite different from abortion. What about the morning-after pill? IUDs? In vitro fertilization? And how about the use of dilation and evacuation or medication for miscarriage management? . . .

Justice Jackson once called a decision he dissented from [Korematsu v. United States (1944)] a "loaded weapon," ready to hand for improper uses. . . . We fear that today's decision, departing from stare decisis for no legitimate reason, is its own loaded weapon. Weakening stare decisis threatens to upend bedrock legal doctrines, far beyond any single decision. Weakening stare decisis creates profound legal instability. And as Casey recognized, weakening stare decisis in a hotly contested case like this one calls into question this Court's commitment to legal principle. It makes the Court appear not restrained but aggressive, not modest but grasping. In all those ways, today's decision takes aim, we fear, at the rule of law. . . .

Now a new and bare majority of this Court—acting at practically the first moment possible—overrules Roe and Casey. It converts a series of dissenting opinions expressing antipathy toward Roe and Casey into a decision greenlighting even total abortion bans. It eliminates a 50-year-old constitutional right that safeguards women's freedom and equal station. It breaches a core rule-of-law principle, designed to promote constancy in the law. In doing all of that, it places in jeopardy other rights, from contraception to same-sex intimacy and marriage. And finally, it undermines the Court's legitimacy. . . .

With sorrow—for this Court, but more, for the many millions of American women who have today lost a fundamental constitutional protection—we dissent. (National Constitution Center, 2024)

Responses from Political Leaders

Responses from political leaders to the overturning of *Roe v. Wade* generally fell along party lines, with well-known Republicans praising the verdict and well-known Democrats decrying the verdict and calling on supporters to have their voices on the issue heard through voting. On the day the verdict was announced, Democratic president Joe Biden told the country in a live announcement:

Today the Supreme Court of the United States expressly took away a constitutional right from the American people that it had already recognized.

This is a sad day for the country in my view. But it doesn't mean the fight's over. Let me be very clear and unambiguous: the only way we can secure a woman's right to choose a balance that exists is for Congress to restore the protections of Roe v. Wade as federal law.

Voters need to make their voices heard. This fall [they] must elect more senators and representatives who will codify a woman's right to choose into federal law once again. (Reuters, 2022)

Democratic Speaker of the House Nancy Pelosi said:

This cruel ruling is outrageous and heart-wrenching. But make no mistake: the rights of women and all Americans are on the ballot this November. (Reuters, 2022)

Republican Senate Minority Leader Mitch McConell released a statement, saying:

This is an historic victory for the Constitution and for the most vulnerable in our society. [The decision is] courageous and correct. (Reuters, 2022)

Former Republican president Donald Trump, who had taken credit for the overturning of *Roe v. Wade* through his appointment of pro-life judges, said:

This is following the Constitution, and giving rights back when they should have been given long ago. . . . This brings everything back to the states where it has always belonged. (Reuters, 2022)

Former Republican vice president Mike Pence wrote:

Today, Life Won. By overturning Roe v. Wade, the Supreme Court of the United States has given the American people a new beginning for life, and I commend the justices in the majority for having the courage of their convictions. (Reuters, 2022)

Former Democratic president Barack Obama said:

Today, the Supreme Court not only reversed nearly 50 years of precedent, it relegated the most intensely personal decision someone can make to the whims of politicians and ideologues—attacking the essential freedoms of millions of Americans. (Reuters, 2022)

Former Democratic secretary of state Hillary Clinton gave the following statement:

Most Americans believe the decision to have a child is one of the most sacred decisions there is, and that such decisions should remain between patients and their doctors. Today's Supreme Court opinion will live in infamy as a step backward for women's rights and human rights. (Reuters, 2022)

Political leaders around the world also weighed in on the historic verdict in the United States. British Prime Minister Boris Johnson said at a news conference:

I think it's a big step backwards. . . . I've always believed in a woman's right to choose and I stick to that view and that is why the UK has the laws that it does. (Reuters, 2022)

On Twitter, French president Emmanuel Macron wrote:

Abortion is a fundamental right for all women. We must protect it. I would like to express my solidarity with all those women whose freedoms have today been compromised by the U.S. Supreme Court. (Reuters, 2022)

Canadian prime minister Justin Trudeau also offered a response on Twitter, writing:

The news coming out of the United States is horrific. My heart goes out to the millions of American women who are now set to lose their legal right to an abortion. . . . No government, politician, or man should tell a woman what she can and cannot do with her body. (Reuters, 2022)

Responses from the Public

Pew Research Center (2022) surveyed the opinions of Americans shortly after the Supreme Court's ruling (between June 27 and July 4, 2022), finding that the majority of Americans disapproved of the decision. Sixty-two percent of those surveyed said they believe abortion should be legal in all (29 percent) or almost all (33 percent) cases. Conversely, 36 percent of those surveyed said abortion should be illegal in all (8 percent) or most cases (28 percent). Pew Research Center polling noted that these numbers did not change notably since their polling before the verdict, in March of 2022.

Perhaps unsurprisingly, public opinions generally also fell along party lines, with 82 percent of Democrats and Independents who lean toward Democratic disapproving of the ruling and 70 percent of Republicans and Independents who lean toward Republican approving of the ruling (Pew Research Center, 2022). According to a survey in late June/early July of 2022, 45 percent of Democrats said they think abortion should be legal in all cases, which was a 7 percentage point increase from Democrats surveyed in March of 2022. Polling found no change in Republicans' views before and after the verdict, with 60 percent saying they think abortion should be illegal in most or all cases (Pew Research Center, 2022). Sixty-three percent of Republican women and 76 percent of Republicans said they approve of the Supreme Court's decision, compared to 81 percent of Democratic women and 83 percent of Democratic men who said they disapprove of the decision (Pew Research Center, 2022).

A greater percentage of women (62 percent, 47 percent strongly) than men (52 percent, 37 percent strongly) said they disapprove of the verdict. Sixty-six percent of women polled said abortion should be legal in most or all cases compared to 57 percent of men (Pew Research Center, 2022). With regard to race, 78 percent of Asian adults, 71 percent of Black adults, 61 percent of Hispanic adults, and 60 percent of white adults responded that they think abortion should be legal in most or all cases. Differences in opinion were also seen among age groups and education levels. Younger adults were more supportive of legal abortion than older adults. Seventy percent of Americans between the ages of eighteen and twenty-nine said abortion should be legal in all or most cases compared to 64 percent of people between the ages of thirty and forty-nine and 57 percent of people aged fifty or older. Seventy-two percent of Americans with postgraduate degrees said they think abortion should be legal in most cases, as did 65 percent of Americans with college degrees, compared to 55 percent of Americans with a high school degree or less education (Pew Research Center, 2022).

Religion also impacted responses to the ruling. Seventy-seven percent of religiously unaffiliated adults said they disapprove of the verdict, 63 percent of whom said they strongly disapprove (Pew Research Center, 2022). Eighty-three percent of religiously unaffiliated adults said they believe abortion should be legal in all or most cases. Fifty-one percent of Catholics said they disapprove of the Court's verdict, with 60 percent saying they think abortion should be legal in all or most cases. Overall, Protestants were divided in their views, with 48 percent saying abortion should be legal in all or most cases and 50 percent saying abortion should be illegal in all or most cases (Pew Research Center, 2022).

In the twenty states (plus the District of Columbia) where abortions were, at the time of polling, legal through at least twenty-four weeks of pregnancy, 65 percent said they disapprove of the court's decision (Pew Research Center, 2022). Fifty-two percent of people in states where, at the time of polling, new gestational restrictions were in effect or set to soon take effect, said they disapprove of the verdict.

Research has also examined public sentiment across social media websites such as X (formerly known as Twitter), Instagram, and Facebook, all of which saw significant increases in activity relating to women's rights, health care, and privacy after the verdict was announced (Mane et al., 2022; Swanson et al, 2022). One study found that, as of September 2022, the majority of the most popular posts related to reproductive rights on TikTok leaned on pro-choice (Pleasure et al., 2024). Conversely, of the fifteen million partisan interactions counted on Facebook on the day of the Dobbs decision, 52 percent (7.7 million) were from right-leaning, pro-life pages. In an analysis of over ten million unique tweets on X from January 1, 2020, to October 17, 2022, a significant decrease in trust in clinicians and health information was observed following the leak of the Supreme Court decision. Initially, terms like "doctor," "physician," and "OB" were associated with trust, but, after May 2, 2022, all terms became negatively correlated with trust (McMann et al., 2024).

A significant increase in searches for contraceptive services on X was also found following the verdict. One study collected and analyzed 166,799 unique tweets related to the marketing of abortion pills, medical simulations, and discussion of home abortions: 92.30 percent of those tweets were made six months after the overturning of *Roe v. Wade*, while only 7.7 percent were from the two years prior (McMann et al., 2024). The surge in demand for contraceptive services was confirmed by Google Trends analysis and a scoping review of the existing literature on the topic. A Google trend analysis conducted between April 6, 2022, and June 5, 2022, showed a statistically significant increase in interest in varying contraceptive methods. Of greatest interest was the search for "vasectomy," which increased 7.14 times, "tubal ligation" 5.89 times, "IUD" 1.8 times, "condom" 1.75 times, and "birth control pill" 1.57 times during this period (Datta et al., 2022). A scoping review of eighteen relevant studies from eight bibliographic databases also confirmed increased demand for contraceptive services (Zhur et al., 2024).

Posts on X also highlighted racial and ethnic disparities exacerbated by the Dobbs decision. The Frontier in Global Women's Health posted a study screening nearly three million tweets related to the overturning of *Roe v. Wade*. Using advanced natural language processing techniques, they found that .7 percent, or 23,044 tweets, discussed the different impact of the decision with regards to race and ethnicity. Sixty percent of these tweets had a negative sentiment. Notably, 11.3 percent of the tweets regarded "racial resentment," while 7.9 percent discussed the decision's impact on "human rights," and 7.4 percent highlighted "socioeconomic disadvantage" (Ujah et al., 2023).

Many X users recognized *Roe v. Wade* as a privacy issue and perceived its overturning as a threat to an individual's private health information. Of 867,546 tweets retrieved during an eight-month study, 646 unique tweets were found to be the most relevant to privacy concerns. Moreover, 180 of those tweets recognized *Roe v. Wade* as a landmark case that protected the privacy of those seeking contraceptive services. Additionally, 162 of the tweets expressed concern that the verdict would lead to other freedoms being taken away, such as marriage rights, gender-affirming care, and even gun rights. Other points of concern highlighted in the study included fear of prosecution and criminalization for abortion-seeking services, the negative impact on rights to bodily autonomy, concerns that personal information may be released to the public, and anxiety regarding the tracking of personal data across websites and apps (Guo et al., 2024).

Responses from Professional Organizations

A number of professional organizations released public statements following the reversal of *Roe v. Wade*. Below are the statements released by the American

Counseling Association. These statements voiced opposition to the Supreme Court's decision, with most organizations stating that the ruling will exacerbate the country's mental health crisis. Many organizations also noted how negative effects of the verdict will disproportionately impact people in marginalized populations.

The American Counseling Association (2022) wrote the following on their website, with the title "American Counseling Association Expresses Opposition to Overturn of Roe v. Wade":

The Supreme Court decision striking down Roe v. Wade abolishes women's constitutional right to choose to have an abortion without the undue influence of government. This decision will trigger some state regulations, which will make abortions outright illegal and/or limiting accessibility. Various jurisdictions have proposed laws and regulations that require clinicians report clients who have sought or are seeking an abortion, as it may be considered "aiding and abetting."

We recognize that the loss of access to safe, legal abortion may hinder the ability of women to participate within the workplace and society effectively and successfully. Unwanted pregnancies may affect women's education, employment, earning prospects, and health. These effects would disproportionately fall on those who are already marginalized, those living in poverty, people of color, nonbinary, and transgender people, as well as those who live in medically underserved areas (e.g., few primary care providers, high infant mortality, high poverty).

Overturning Roe v. Wade means we can expect an increase in economic hardship and insecurity that may lead to increased stress, lower life satisfaction, decreased work productivity, increased turnover, and decreased mental well-being. Professional counselors assist clients and students facing life's challenges such as the deeply personal decision to have an abortion, and how to access such services.

The American Counseling Association (ACA) stands with every person, counselor, and client in pursuit of mental health care and wellness. Professional counselors are being placed in an unethical position. In counseling, clients are entitled to self-determination and to make decisions in the best interest of their health and well-being. Clients should have access to high-quality professional counseling without the fear of having their confidentiality unjustly waived. This requires safeguarding the integrity and trust built in the counselor-client relationship.

Professional counselors need to continue to practice ethically and obtain a legal consultation to determine their duty to confidentiality and privacy versus the conflict either in Roe v. Wade or the restrictions their state has put in place. Professional counselors may request an opinion from their State Attorney General who can give an official interpretation of the law. (American Counseling Association, 2022)

The American Psychological Association (APA, 2022b) released the below press release, titled "APA decries SCOTUS decision on abortion," which included quotes from the organization's president:

American Psychological Association expressed deep concern and profound disappointment in response to the U.S. Supreme Court's decision eliminating the constitutional right to abortion.

"This ruling ignores not only precedent but science, and will exacerbate the mental health crisis America is already experiencing," said APA President Frank C. Worrell, PhD. "We are alarmed that the justices would nullify Roe despite decades of scientific research demonstrating that people who are denied abortions are more likely to experience higher levels of anxiety, lower life satisfaction and lower self-esteem compared with those who are able to obtain abortions."

"A person's ability to control when and if they have a child is frequently linked to their socioeconomic standing and earning power. Therefore, restricting access to safe, legal abortions is most likely to affect those living in poverty, people of color, and sexual and gender identity minorities, as well as those who live in rural or medically underserved areas."

Pushing decisions regarding the legality of abortion to the states guarantees that an untold number of people will no longer be able to access the procedure, he said. "And the fact that at least 13 states have 'trigger laws' automatically implementing abortion restrictions puts people in immediate jeopardy," Worrell said.

Research also suggests that adding barriers to accessing abortion services may increase symptoms of stress, anxiety and depression, according to Worrell.

"The number of unsafe abortions is likely to increase as a result of this decision," Worrell said.

Research also demonstrates a strong relationship between unwanted pregnancy and interpersonal violence. Specifically, psychological science suggests that the inability to obtain an abortion increases the risk for domestic abuse among those who are forced to stay in contact with violent partners, putting them and their children at risk.

Finally, Worrell noted that by eliminating the constitutional right to privacy, the Supreme Court is opening the door to curtailing other rights, including the right to obtain contraception legally and same-sex marriage—both of which APA supports based on the scientific research showing their denial can have negative mental health impacts.

APA has long been a strong and consistent voice for equal access to reproductive health services. The association has passed four policies or resolutions since 1969 affirming a woman's right to choose and negating assertions regarding the alleged adverse psychological effects of abortion. APA has also filed 11 amicus curiae briefs in cases involving abortion. The most recent policy (PDF, 72KB) was passed in February 2022. (APA, 2022b)

The American Mental Health Counselors Association (AMHCA) released a formal announcement stating the following:

> The recent overturning of Roe V Wade has majorly impacted many people and CMHCs [Clinical Mental Health Counselors] throughout the United States. We respect that the recent ruling can contribute to people feeling concerned for the future and worried about their bodily autonomy. AMHCA is committed to women's rights and advocates for safe and secure medical treatment which is agreed upon by individuals and their medical doctors. We denounce any attempts to limit human rights and promote a fair and equitable society. As this issue is a divisive topic, we remain committed to our ethical standards to not impose our own personal beliefs onto those we serve. We also remain committed in our approach to clinical treatment through a perspective of cultural humility to meet clients where they are at and work with them on their goals. (Meyerhoeffer, 2022)

The American Association for Marriage and Family Therapy's (AAMFT, 2022) statement on the overturning of *Roe v. Wade* read:

> Access to medically safe abortion has been a fabric of society in the United States for fifty years. And in one day that changed in many parts of our

country. The Supreme Court's recent decision to overturn Roe v. Wade has invoked passionate and complex feelings in Americans ranging from sadness and fear to relief and satisfaction. And these complicated feelings are playing themselves out in our relationships, our families, and our communities, often further dividing an already polarized society. Therapists are navigating these feelings both personally and with their clients as a vital support system.

Abortion is a highly complicated issue, with complex facets, for which many Americans agree there is no easy answer. However, there is no doubt that the ramifications of this legal change will most heavily impact low-income as well as marginalized segments of our population in a disproportionate way. Once again, these people most harshly bear the burden of barriers for access to care in this country.

As an organization that believes in the vitality of relationships, the strength of grassroots advocacy, and the power of fair representation we encourage you to take this time to share your thoughts with your elected representatives to ensure your voice is heard. During this time, AAMFT is committed to supporting our member therapists as they navigate the legal and ethical challenges, as well as the necessary training to support their clients, as a result of this ruling and any subsequent legislation or decisions. (AAMFT, 2022)

The National Association of Social Workers (NASW, 2022) issued the below press release, titled "NASW Condemns Decision by the U.S. Supreme Court to Overturn Roe v. Wade," on the day of the Supreme Court ruling:

The National Association of Social Workers (NASW) condemns today's U.S. Supreme Court decision ruling in the Mississippi case of Dobbs v. Jackson Women's Health Organization that effectively overturns Roe v. Wade.

This decision is not only the first time the Court has taken away a recognized individual liberty, it also decimates the nearly 50-year precedent that established abortion rights as an extension of the implied Right to Privacy found in the 14th Amendment.

With this ruling, the Court is allowing Mississippi to enforce its 15-week ban on abortion and is inviting eager state legislatures to further restrict and ban abortion. In many states, these restrictive measures will even go so far as to criminalize providers—including social workers—who may simply be doing their jobs by supporting a pregnant person in making decisions regarding reproductive care.

This decision is an unconscionable rollback of fundamental rights for all people in the United States. Forced pregnancy is a grave violation of human rights and dignity.

We should all be able to make the personal health care decisions that impact our lives, health, and futures. But the Court today issued a shattering blow to access to abortion in the United States, leaving even more people struggling to obtain essential health care. The abortion ban will also disproportionately affect people of color, who already have less access to reproductive care. In fact, abortion bans like Mississippi's are part of intertwined systems of oppression that deny many vulnerable people access to their rights.

Besides people of color, the impact of this decision will also fall heavily on people with disabilities, people who live in rural areas, young people, undocumented people, and people who are low income. With this decision, the U.S. Supreme Court has once again failed the most disadvantaged Americans.

Decades of attacks have left abortion rights hanging by a thread in the United States. Today that thread was cut, but we are not defeated. Anti-abortion state lawmakers are already trying to prohibit people from accessing abortion across state lines, showing there's no limit to their cruel attempts to control people's personal health care decisions. These laws must be stopped.

NASW upholds that all individuals have a right to bodily autonomy, that abortion is health care, and that all individuals have the right to freedom of choice in accessing essential health care services, especially their reproductive health. Despite today's decision, NASW will continue to advocate for reproductive rights for all on the local, state, and federal level. (NASW, 2022)

In addition to the statement issued by the NASW, at least one state chapter of the NASW put out its own statement (NASW North Carolina Chapter, 2022). There were also statements authored by the Council on Social Work Education (CSWE) (2022) and the Society for Social Work Leadership in Healthcare (2024), as well as by a collaboration between the American Psychological Association (APA), the American Psychiatric Association, and the NASW (NASW, 2022b). Several schools of social work also responded publicly to the ruling. The University at Buffalo School of Social Work (2022a) and the University of Washington School of Social Work (2024), in collaboration with its Schools of Nursing and Public Health, issued their own statements. The University at Buffalo School of Social Work (2022b) also put out a podcast focused on social work in the post-Roe world. Virginia Commonwealth University School of Social Work (2023), meanwhile, has highlighted the connections between social work and reproductive justice on a school website aimed at prospective students.

Professional medical organizations also released formal responses to the Supreme Court ruling. In a statement titled *"Ruling an Egregious Allowance of Government Intrusion into Medicine,"* Dr. Jack Resneck, president of the American Medical Association (AMA, 2022), wrote on the organization's behalf:

> The American Medical Association is deeply disturbed by the U.S. Supreme Court's decision to overturn nearly a half century of precedent protecting patients' right to critical reproductive health care—representing an egregious allowance of government intrusion into the medical examination room, a direct attack on the practice of medicine and the patient-physician relationship, and a brazen violation of patients' rights to evidence-based reproductive health services. States that end legal abortion will not end abortion—they will end safe abortion, risking devastating consequences, including patients' lives.
>
> Today's opinion shifting reproductive health decision-making to lawmakers opens a deep political rift between states over access to reproductive health services that places sound medical practice and the health of patients at risk. State restrictions that intrude on the practice of medicine and interfere with the patient-physician relationship leave millions with little or no access to reproductive health services while criminalizing medical care.
>
> Access to legal reproductive care will be limited to those with the sufficient resources, circumstances, and financial means to do so—exacerbating health inequities by placing the heaviest burden on patients from Black, Latinx, Indigenous, low-income, rural, and other historically disadvantaged communities who already face numerous structural and systemic barriers to accessing health care.

In alignment with our long-held position that the early termination of a pregnancy is a medical matter between the patient and physician, subject only to the physician's clinical judgment and the patient's informed consent, the AMA condemns the high court's interpretation in this case. We will always have physicians' backs and defend the practice of medicine, we will fight to protect the patient-physician relationship, and we will oppose any law or regulation that compromises or criminalizes patient access to safe, evidence-based medical care, including abortion. As the health of millions of patients hangs in the balance, this is a fight we will not give up. (AMA, 2022)

The American Academy of Child and Adolescent Psychiatry (2022) released the below statement on the day of the Supreme Court's ruling to overturn *Roe v. Wade*:

The American Academy of Child and Adolescent Psychiatry (AACAP) is disappointed, saddened, and outraged by today's U.S. Supreme Court's decision in Dobbs v. Jackson Women's Health Organization, effectively overturning Roe v. Wade, thereby restricting an individual's right to an abortion.

Research clearly shows that those denied an abortion experience lasting negative impacts to their health, especially mental health, and overall well-being. As a result of today's decision, women now face a terrifying landscape when trying to access the care they need that will undoubtedly put the health of millions of women at risk. This is especially true with vulnerable and marginalized populations.

Youth with mental disorders are a vulnerable population. Lack of abortion availability for pregnant teens with psychiatric disorders may severely impact the course of their health, including mental health and increase risk for suicide. The Supreme Court's ruling, in combination with state laws criminalizing support or assistance to these youth seeking abortions can criminalize psychiatric care, impeding our ability as child and adolescent psychiatrists, to act in the best interests of our patient's overall health care needs.

AACAP reaffirms our commitment to work with all of organized medicine in advocating that health care is a basic human right, and all aspects of health care must be considered, protected, and safeguarded. AACAP also reaffirms the sanctity of the physician-patient relationship. (AACAP, 2022)

The Group of Six (2022), an organization that represents medical doctors in various fields in the United States, published the below press release, coauthored by the American Academy of Family Physicians, American Academy of Pediatrics, American College of Obstetricians and Gynecologists, American College of Physicians, and American Psychiatric Association:

> Our organizations, representing over 400,000 physicians and medical students, condemn the Supreme Court decision in Dobbs v. Jackson Women's Health Organization, striking down the protections afforded to people in need of abortion care for five decades. (Group of Six, 2022)

Actions in Response to the Verdict

Both abortion rights activists and anti-abortion activists continued their efforts after the overturning of *Roe v. Wade*. As described in Chapter 1, opponents of abortion were successful in having a number of regulations passed in states to restrict abortions following the Supreme Court verdict. In thirteen states, opponents of abortion were poised for a reversal of *Roe v. Wade* and had laws called "trigger laws" in place for such an occasion. These laws automatically banned abortion under most, if not all, circumstances once Roe was overturned (Whitesell, 2024). Anti-abortion activists in other states, such as Tennessee and Louisiana, which have some of the strictest trigger laws in the country at the time of writing, have also mobilized their supporters since the verdict to help ensure that state legislatures do not weaken these laws (Whitesell, 2024).

Conversely, following the Supreme Court decision, abortion rights advocates were motivated to elect Democratic legislators across the country and to suppress abortion-related ballot measures. Abortion rights supporters won all six abortion-related ballot measures in the 2022 midterm elections and helped elect many Democrats around the country (Littlefield, 2023). In Pennsylvania, outrage over the verdict helped Democrats flip the state House, elect a Democratic governor, and elect pro-choice Democrat John Fetterman to the US Senate (Littlefield, 2023).

Reproductive issues were also a key issue in the 2024 Presidential election, with Democratic candidate Kamala Harris blaming Republican candidate Donald Trump for the reversal of Roe and warning he would further restrict abortion rights if elected to a second term. Despite Trump applauding and taking credit for the overturning of Roe, on the 2024 presidential campaign trail, he softened his stance, stating that he would not sign a national abortion ban (Lee, 2024). Similarly, Trump's running mate J. D. Vance previously supported banning abortion with no exceptions but ended up aligning himself with Trump's position to leave the issue up to the states (Lee, 2024). Trump's tempered position could have possibly been due to the polling at the time showing Americans' large support for legal abortion (Lee, 2024). Trump ultimately won the 2024 Presidential election, sweeping all seven battleground states. Notably, despite Trump's statement that he would not sign a federal ban on abortion, many reproductive rights advocates expressed significant fear after he was reelected. Brittany Fonteno, president of the National Abortion Federation, an organization representing doctors and clinics that provide abortions, said at the time that she expected a second Trump administration to be "devastating for abortion rights and access" (Broden & Nadworny, 2024, para. 8). Nancy Northup, president and CEO of the Center for Reproductive Rights, similarly called Trump's election "a deadly threat to . . . reproductive rights" (Center for Reproductive Rights, 2024, para. 1). Northup cited concerns that Trump would

> seek to stop the availability of medication abortion by mail, which has been a lifeline in post-Roe America. It will attempt to gag all organizations, including U.S.-based ones, from advocating for abortion law reform or providing abortion care abroad, even with their non-U.S. funds. It will push policies designed to disempower reproductive and human rights organizations while aiding their anti-rights counterparts. Such attacks at the federal level will reverberate in the states, undoubtedly leading to more prosecutions, investigations, and lawsuits against providers, patients, and their loved ones. (Center for Reproductive Rights, 2024, para. 3)

Among the public, sales of abortion pills and Plan B soared following the 2024 Presidential election, likely also due to concerns that access to these medications could become prohibited or illegal under Donald Trump (Broden & Nadworny, 2024). An increased demand for emergency contraceptives was previously seen following the Dobbs decision, with demand for Restart, a morning-after pill manufactured by Stix, increasing by more than 600 percent in the twenty-four hours after the verdict (Rosman & Cherelus, 2022). Some of the people who purchased emergency contraceptives at the time said that doing so gave them a sense of control or power in the face of fears and uncertainty regarding possible restrictions on contraception (Rosman & Cherelus, 2022).

Finally, a number of professional organizations have backed up their statements decrying the overturning of *Roe v. Wade* with advocacy efforts. For example, the AMA (AMA, 2024) has engaged in a number of advocacy actions following the verdict. In an Advocacy in Action brief released by the organization in May 2024, the AMA indicated that they have

Supported continued, unrestricted access to mifepristone through joint letters with the American College of Obstetricians and Gynecologists to the White House and the Food and Drug Administration.

Supported new Department of Health and Human Services privacy guidance making it clear that physicians are not required to disclose private medical information to third parties and providing patients with tips on the use of personal cell phones and tablets.

Submitted testimony to the House Committee on Energy and Commerce Subcommittee on Oversight and Investigations as part of its hearing, "Roe Reversal: The Impacts of Taking Away the Constitutional Right to an Abortion."

Joined the American College of Obstetricians and Gynecologists and more than 75 other medical professional societies in voicing unified opposition to legislative interference in the relationship between patients, physicians and other health professionals.

Applauded President Joe Biden's executive order pledging to explore pathways to protect access to reproductive health care services.

Supported the Biden administration's guidance on the Emergency Medical Treatment and Labor Act superseding state bans on abortions and has filed amicus briefs in Texas v. Becerra and United States v. Idaho on the topic.

Issued statement with American Pharmacists Association, American Society of Health-System Pharmacists and National Community Pharmacists Association calling on policymakers to clarify legal obligations related to prescribing/ dispensing medications that are indicated for abortion but may be prescribed for other reasons (i.e., methotrexate).

Filed a number of amicus briefs challenging state bans on abortion, including in Arizona. (AMA, 2024)

Regarding the ongoing actions they are taking, the AMA (2024) wrote that they were

Encouraging the administration and Justice Department to ensure patients can travel freely across state lines to get abortions when they can't in their own states, and that physicians who treat them won't be attacked by zealous prosecutors in restrictive states.

Working to get the FDA to make oral hormonal contraceptives available over the counter.

Collaborating with state medical associations to ensure access to medically necessary care and laws to protect abortion providers and patients from cross-state criminal and civil actions. (AMA, 2024)

The APA (2022a) has a long history of supporting reproductive rights, dating to 1969, when the organization's council passed a resolution asserting that terminating a pregnancy should be a legal right if performed by a licensed physician in a licensed medical facility. In 1989, the APA (2022a) identified freedom of reproductive choice as a mental health and child welfare issue. Like the AMA, the APA (2022a) has also filed numerous amicus briefs in support of reproductive rights in a variety of cases, including *Thornburgh v. American College of Obstetricians and Gynecologists, Harris v. McRae, Bowen v. Kendrick,* and *Akron v. Akron Center for Reproductive Health*. The APA (2022a) reaffirmed its support for legal access to legal abortion in the months preceding the Dobbs decision. In the days preceding the verdict, APA members and staff held a briefing and listening session on reproductive rights featuring experts in reproductive health.

Stefanie Reeves (personal communication, July 16, 2024), deputy chief of Public Policy and Engagement, Advocacy Directorate for the APA, provided information to the authors of this book about the numerous advocacy activities the APA has engaged in following the Dobbs decision. Immediately after the verdict, the APA held a virtual town hall attended by approximately 500 members which focused on the legal implications for practitioners. After the town hall, they provided additional guidance and resources for members, held discussions with key constituents about needs and concerns, and continued to monitor and coordinate with APA Services and State Psychological Associations on any proposed state laws that could directly impact practitioners. In July 2022, APA Services sent an action alert asking APA members to call their representatives in support of HR 8296, the Women's Health Protection Act of 2022 sponsored by Rep. Judy Chu and HR 8297, and the Ensuring Women's Right to Reproductive Freedom Act introduced by Rep. Lizzie Fletcher. HR 8296 prohibits governmental restrictions on the provision of, and access to, abortion services, while HR 8297 prohibits anyone acting under state law from interfering with a person's ability to access out-of-state abortion services. Both bills passed the House on July 15, 2022. That same month, APA Services provided members with a list of resources to congressional committees hosting hearings on reproductive health, met with leaders of the Maternal Mental Health Leadership Alliance to discuss possible collaboration on reproductive health efforts, developed a resource page for members interested in engaging in reproductive health advocacy efforts, and hosted a virtual state advocacy training session with over 600 registrants. In August, reproductive rights were discussed at their annual conference, and in October APA staff participated in a virtual symposium titled "Reproductive Justice: Human Rights, Equity and Advocacy hosted by the University of South Florida" (Reeves, personal communication, July 16, 2024).

In early 2023, APA Council voted in the affirmative for a new policy on confidentiality and reproductive health which reaffirmed the psychologist's ability to keep a patient's discussion on reproductive health confidential (Reeves, personal communication, July 16, 2024). APA Services also endorsed the Women's Health Protection Act (H.R. 12/S. 701), which prohibits governmental restrictions on the provision of, and access to, abortion services, and requires immediately providing abortion services if delaying risks the patient's health. Additionally in 2023, APA Services participated in an interdivisional meeting where issues that developed after the overturning of Roe were discussed, including rejection of funding for research projects centered on reproductive health and where postdoctoral interns would go for internships. Additionally, they submitted comments to the Department of Health and Human Services on modifications to HIPAA to protect privacy and reproductive health. Per Reeves (personal communication, July 16, 2024), comments were in line with APA Council policies affirming the support for access to reproductive health services and the need for maintaining privacy of information related to reproductive health. They also endorsed the Right to Contraception Act (H.R. 4121/S. 1999), which protects a person's ability to access contraception as well as a provider's ability to provide products, services, and information related to contraception.

APA advocacy efforts continued in 2024. In January that year, APA was invited to participate in a listening session led by Dr. Carolyn Mazure, an APA member and chair of the White House Initiative on Women's Health Research (Reeves, personal communication, July 16, 2024). After receiving comprehensive comments from several APA members, led by Division 38, APA followed up with written comments, which included recommending that the White House advance research on the consequences of denying access to safe and legal pregnancy termination, including mental health outcomes, promote research on causal factors associated with Black women's maternal morbidity, and research early identification of persons at risk for postpartum suicide, and the development of effective interventions tailored to communities. Throughout the year, APA and APA Services have shared psychological science on reproductive health with members of Congress, federal agencies, and external community partners, advocated for increased funding for maternal health services, and utilized APA's Council policies on reproductive health to engage partners in the reproductive health space (Reeves, personal communication, July 16, 2024).

When reached for comment for this text, Guila Todd (personal communication, July 15, 2024), director of Government Affairs and Public Policy for the American Counseling Association, said the following:

> While ACA has issued a statement regarding the Dobbs decision, the bulk of our advocacy efforts have centered on maternal mental health and significantly bolstering behavioral health services for mothers in need. While we remain open to discussions about the Dobbs legislation, our primary focus in advocacy has not currently shifted in that direction.

With regard to advocacy actions taken by professional social work organizations, the NASW and several of its state chapters organized educational activities related to the changing realities of the field since the fall of Roe. A prominent section of the NASW's website now focuses on reproductive justice, with videos, news releases, and links providing information about related policies and advocacy opportunities (NASW, 2024). The New York state chapter organized a series of two town hall meetings focused on social work and reproductive rights (NASW New York State Chapter, n.d.). The New Jersey chapter shared a video presentation on YouTube focused on social work ethics given the changing context of reproductive rights in the United States (NASW New Jersey, 2022). Similarly, the Virginia chapter has offered a workshop about working with clients who have had abortions, taking into account the professional's own values as well as legal and ethical considerations (NASW, n.d.).

Social work scholars and practitioners have also worked to disseminate information about social work practice after Dobbs by writing about related topics. Social workers have penned articles that have been published in a variety of academic journals and professional publications related to social work practice (Barsky, 2022; Cheney & Rotabi, 2024; Poehling et al., 2023; Reamer, 2023). Beyond this, the NASW and several of its chapters have gotten involved in activism and legislative advocacy aimed at protecting reproductive rights. These efforts started prior to the Dobbs ruling in response to growing concerns regarding reproductive rights at the state and national levels. In 2021, in protest of Senate Bill 8, the recently passed Texas legislation that banned abortion after six weeks gestation—and with an eye to trying to protect abortion rights at the national level—the NASW signed on as part of a coalition to organize the Women's March to Mobilize and Defend Our Reproductive Rights. This event included a primary march in Washington, D.C. as well as smaller marches in hundreds of cities around the United States (NASW, 2021).

Meanwhile, the NASW Legal Defense Fund has joined amicus briefs in reproductive rights cases which in recent years have included *Cochran v. Gresham, Dobbs v. Jackson Women's Health Organization,* and *Whole Women's Health v. Jackson.* Related to the latter case, the NASW Texas Chapter was also highly involved in opposing Texas's Senate Bill 8 by educating and mobilizing its members and working in coalition with other groups (NASW, 2022a). However, these efforts were unable to prevent the passage of this bill into Texas state law. Similarly, the NASW and many of its state chapters have been actively engaged in efforts related to other proposed legislation concerning abortion. These activities have included the dissemination of informational materials and action alerts to members and promoting social worker involvement in legislative advocacy and voting. There have also been many instances of collaboration between the NASW and local and national organizations that are actively involved in reproductive health care and the protection of reproductive rights. In two notable instances that occurred prior to or around the time of the Dobbs decision, statewide chapters of the NASW have been actively involved in successful initiatives related to reproductive rights in their areas. In Massachusetts, starting in 2019, the NASW Massachusetts Chapter joined a statewide coalition of more than seventy groups, led by the Planned Parenthood Advocacy Fund of Massachusetts, NARAL Pro-Choice Massachusetts, and the ACLU of Massachusetts. Through this campaign, advocates drafted an act to Remove Obstacles and Expand Abortion Access, or the ROE Act, and worked with key legislators to file the act (Gewirtz, 2022). Eventually, key provisions of the original act moved forward in a pared-down form as a budget amendment. In December of 2020, Governor Charlie Parker vetoed the legislation, but the governor's veto was then quickly overridden by votes in the Massachusetts state House and Senate. The passed legislation removed the requirement for parental consent for sixteen- and seventeen-year-olds, expanded access to abortion care after twenty-four weeks gestation for those who receive a diagnosis that would be fatal to the fetus, and enshrined into state law the affirmative right to abortion (Baker, 2020; Romo, 2020).

Finally, in 2022, NASW Ohio and the Abortion Fund of Ohio (formerly known as Women Have Options Ohio), represented by the ACLU of Ohio and Democracy Forward, filed a federal lawsuit challenging an abortion ban that was adopted by Lebanon City Council in 2021. This lawsuit, *National Association of Social Workers et al. v. City of Lebanon, Ohio, et al.*, was dropped when the city amended the language in the law to no longer criminalize those who assist Lebanon residents in seeking abortion care outside of the city

(NASW, 2023). Though the law continued to prohibit abortion clinics from operating within city limits, there were no abortion clinics located in Lebanon at the time, and there were no known plans to change that (Ingles, 2023). At the time that the lawsuit was dropped in 2022, reproductive rights advocates in Ohio planned to propose an amendment to the state constitution in the future, codifying the right to abortion (Ingles, 2023). The following year, in November 2023, a majority of Ohio voters approved a ballot measure that led to the passage of a constitutional amendment enshrining the right to abortion into Ohio state law (Smyth, 2023). Based on the implementation of this amendment, abortion rights in the state of Ohio were restored.

According to Danielle Smith (personal communication, November 18, 2024), executive director of NASW Ohio, the chapter has been involved in advocating for abortion rights and reproductive justice for more than twenty years. The chapter became involved in opposing the Lebanon ordinance after Smith and chapter members learned that it included language that criminalized "abortion doula services," which the city defined as providing "emotional, logistical, or informational support in accessing abortion"—roles that members realized could be applied to social workers and other health and mental health professionals. The chapter developed an impact statement that was used in the lawsuit based on interviews with close to 100 social workers who worked in Lebanon or had clients who lived there. The suit had the distinction of being the first abortion rights legal action in the country following the Dobbs decision. When asked what helped make this campaign effective, Smith (personal communication, November 18, 2024) noted the natural role of social workers in reproductive rights advocacy. This connection is based on the social work focus on meeting clients "where they're at" while working in a wide range of settings, including mental health, health care, and child welfare. She also cited the networks that social workers had already developed in communities across the state, enabling them to relatively easily gather information, work in partnership across disciplines, and mobilize when needed. Through this campaign, Smith (personal communication, November 18, 2024) and members of the chapter developed a better understanding of how many social workers were already talking with their clients about their clients' reproductive health care decisions. They found that many social workers were so committed to doing right by their clients in "holding space for them to process their emotions and make their own decisions" about their health care and their lives that they felt compelled to continue this work, regardless of legality. This was the case even for some social workers who were personally opposed to abortion but who viewed the Lebanon ordinance as "infringing on their ability to help their clients." They also found that, for many social workers, these issues were less political than some may think, instead ultimately coming down to the rights of health care providers and those they serve. Similarly, many members reported that these topics were less divisive than they had feared and that their involvement in this campaign did not damage their partnerships with organizations and legislators who are opposed to abortion. On what she would recommend to mental health professionals who are considering joining efforts to protect reproductive rights, Smith (personal communication, November 18, 2024) emphasized the importance of working with partners who have already been doing this work. She also noted how crucial it is for people and organizations other than reproductive rights organizations to engage in this work, demonstrating the true depth and breadth of the importance of reproductive rights. She also encouraged those who care about reproductive rights to boldly take that first step in getting more involved, saying "testify, support initiatives, and don't be afraid of the consequences." She also spoke of reasons to maintain hope, noting that the Ohio ballot initiative passed by a wide margin, even in a state that can be politically conservative and which has often been a battleground when it comes to reproductive rights. Smith reflected on how things have changed since the time of the vote. For years, individuals seeking abortion care had been forced to leave Ohio to seek these services; currently, it's the other way around. During a panel discussion at the chapter's recent conference, several participants spoke of helping people from other states come to Ohio when they were seeking abortions.

Conclusion

A combination of factors led to the landmark *Roe v. Wade* ruling being reversed. The reversal was followed by a diverse spectrum of reactions from various sectors, including political figures, the general public, and prominent professional organizations. Key steps in understanding these responses include examining the motivations and rhetoric employed by leaders on both sides of the debate, as well as the grassroots mobilization efforts that surged in the aftermath. The ruling had profound impacts on the national discourse surrounding reproductive rights, illustrating how it has reshaped both legislative agendas and public sentiment.

Discussion Questions

1) What was your personal reaction/response to the overturning of *Roe v. Wade*? What were the reactions/responses of people you know both personally and professionally?
2) Why do you think professional organizations responded to the ruling in the ways they did?
3) In addition to the responses detailed in this chapter, what other statements or actions were taken by various entities following the overturning of *Roe v. Wade*?

References

American Academy of Child & Adolescent Psychiatry. (2022, June 24*). AACAP statement on SCOTUS decision overturning Roe v. Wade.* https://www.aacap.org/aacap/zLatest_News/AACAP_Statement_SCOTUS_Decision_Overturning_Roe_v_Wade.aspx

American Association for Marriage and Family Therapy. (2022, June 28). *Statement on Roe v. Wade.* https://blog.aamft.org/2022/06/statement-on-roe-v-wade-.html

American Counseling Association. (2022, June 24). *American counseling association expresses opposition to overturn of Roe v. Wade.* https://www.counseling.org/news/news-detail/2022/06/24/american-counseling-association-expresses-opposition-to-overturn-of-roe-v.-wade

American Psychological Association. (2022a, March 1). *APA reaffirms support for reproductive rights, including access to legal abortion* [Press release]. https://www .apa.org/news/press/releases/2022/03/reproductive-rights

American Psychological Association. (2022b, June 27). *APA decries SCOTUS decision on abortion.* https://www.apa.org/news/press/releases/2022/06/scotus-abortion -decision

American Medical Association. (2024, May 31). *Advocacy in action: Protecting reproductive rights.* https://www.ama-assn.org/delivering-care/public-health/ advocacy-action-protecting-reproductive-health

American Medical Association. (2022, June 24). *Ruling an egregious allowance of government intrusion into medicine.* https://www.ama-assn.org/press-center/press -releases/ruling-egregious-allowance-government-intrusion-medicine#

Baker, C.N. (2020, December 29). Groundbreaking Massachusetts abortion law repeals parental consent for older teens. *Ms. Magazine.* https://msmagazine.com /2020/12/29/massachusetts-abortion-law-roe-act/

Barsky, A. (2022, September). Ethics alive! Abortion care and social work after Dobbs. *The New Social Worker.* https://www.socialworker.com/feature-articles/ ethics-articles/abortion-care-social-work-after-dobbs/

Broden, S., & Nadworny, E. (2024, November 16). Women stock up on abortion pills and Plan B, fearing new restrictions under Trump. *NPR.* https://www.npr.org/ sections/shots-health-news/2024/11/16/nx-s1-5184438/trump-women-abortion -pill-plan-b

Center for Reproductive Rights. (2024, November 06). *Trump Declared Winner of 2024 Presidential Election.* https://reproductiverights.org/trump-declared-winner -of-2024-presidential-election/

Center for Reproductive Rights. (n. d.). *Dobbs v. Jackson Women's Health Organization. The case in depth.* https://reproductiverights.org/case/scotus -mississippi-abortion-ban/dobbs-jackson-womens-health/

Cheney, K., & Rotabi, K. S. (2024). Social work in a post-Dobbs world: The 'adoption fallacy,' decolonization, and reproductive justice. *Affilia, 39*(2), 202–213. https:// doi.org/10.1177/08861099231210941

Council on Social Work Education. (2022, June 24). *CSWE disagrees with decision to overturn Roe v. Wade.* https://www.cswe.org/news/newsroom/cswe-statement-on -overturning-roe-v-wade/

Datta, P., Chowdhury, S., Aravindan, A., Nath, S., & Sen, P. (2022, July 19). Looking for a silver lining to the dark cloud: A google trends analysis of contraceptive interest in the United States Post Roe vs. Wade Verdict. *Cureus,14*(7), e27012. https://pmc.ncbi.nlm.nih.gov/articles/PMC9386304/#

Gewirtz, R. (2022, May 6). Hyperlocal organizing starting now. *Social Work Blog.* https://www.socialworkblog.org/sw-practice/health-care/2022/05/the-roe-act-and -the-path-forward-for-our-nation/

Group of Six. (2022, June 2024). *Physicians: SCOTUS decision jeopardizes patient– physician relationship, penalizes evidence-based care.* http://www.groupof6.org/ content/dam/AAFP/documents/advocacy/prevention/women/ST-G5-SCOTUS -DobbsVJackson-062422.pdf

Guo, Y., Zehrung, R., Genuario, K., Lu, X., Mei, Q., Chen, Y., & Zheng, K. (2024). *Perspectives on privacy in the post-roe era: A mixed-methods of machine learning and qualitative analyses of tweets.* AMIA Annual Symposium Proceedings 2023, pp. 951–960. https://pmc.ncbi.nlm.nih.gov/articles/PMC10785943/

Ingles, J. (2023, January 13). Ohio city relaxes abortion law while abortion rights advocates consider their next moves. *The Statehouse News Bureau.* https://www .statenews.org/government-politics/2023-01-13/ohio-city-relaxes-abortion-law -while-abortion-rights-advocates-consider-their-next-moves

Lee, C. (2024, November 06). What Donald Trump's win means for abortion. *Time.* https://time.com/7096575/donald-trump-abortion-plan-2024/

Littlefield, A. (2023, June 28). The anti-abortion movement gets a dose of post-Roe reality. *The Nation.* https://www.thenation.com/article/politics/anti-abortion -activists-dobbs/

Mane, H., Yue, X., Yu, W., Doig, A. C., Wei, H., Delcid, N., Harris, A. G., Nguyen, T. T., & Nguyen, Q. C. (2022). Examination of the public's reaction on Twitter to the over-turning of Roe v Wade and abortion bans. *Healthcare (Basel, Switzerland), 10*(12), 2390. https://doi.org/10.3390/healthcare10122390

McMann, T. J., Haupt, M. R., Le, N., Meurice, M. E., Li, J., Cuomo, R. E., & Mackey, T. K. (2024). Abortion pill marketing and sourcing on twitter following Dobbs v. Jackson supreme court ruling. *The European Journal of Contraception & Reproductive Health Care: The Official Journal of the European Society of Contraception, 29*(4), 139–144.

Meyerhoeffer, W. (2022, July 07). *Formal Roe v Wade announcement from AMHCA.* American Mental Health Counselors Association. https://www.amhca.org/blogs/ whitney-meyerhoeffer/2022/07/06/formal-roe-v-wade-announcement-from-amhca

NASW New Jersey. (2022, July 22). *Social work ethics in the wake of Roe v Wade Supreme Court decision 7.27.22* [Video]. YouTube. https://youtu.be/P300BQCuICk ?si=7NAKzkyZToyzfhaS

National Association of Social Workers. (2021, September 21). NASW joins march for reproductive rights. *Social Work Blog.* https://www.socialworkblog.org/sw-practice/health-care/2021/09/join-nasws-march-for-reproductive-rights/

National Association of Social Workers. (2022a, May 3). Reproductive rights legal cases handled by the NASW legal defense fund. *Social Work Blog.* https://www.socialworkblog.org/sw-practice/2022/05/reproductive-rights-legal-cases-handled-by-the-nasw-legal-defense-fund/

National Association of Social Workers. (2022b, June 24). *News releases: Major mental health associations decry U.S. Supreme Court decision overturning Roe v. Wade.* https://www.socialworkers.org/News/News-Releases/ID/2504/Major-Mental-Health-Associations-decry-US-Supreme-Court-decision-overturning-Roe-v-Wade

National Association of Social Workers. (2024). *Policy issues: Reproductive rights are human rights.* https://www.socialworkers.org/Advocacy/Policy-Issues/Reproductive-Rights-Are-Human-Rights

National Constitution Center. (2024). *Dobbs v. Jackson Women's Health Organization (2022).* https://constitutioncenter.org/the-constitution/supreme-court-case-library/dobbs-v-jackson-womens-health-organization

Pew Research Center. (2022, July 06). *Majority of publmaneic disapproves of supreme court's decision to overturn Roe v. Wade.* https://www.pewresearch.org/politics/2022/07/06/majority-of-public-disapproves-of-supreme-courts-decision-to-overturn-roe-v-wade/

Pleasure, Z., Becker, A., Johnson, D., Broussard, K., & Lindberg, L. (2024, May). How TikTok is being used to talk about abortion post-Roe: A content analysis of the most liked abortion TikToks. *Contraception, 133,* 110384. https://www.sciencedirect.com/science/article/abs/pii/S0010782424000301

Poehling, C., Downey, M. M., Singh, M. I., & Beasley, C. C. (2023). From gaslighting to enlightening: Reproductive justice as an interdisciplinary solution to close the health gap. *Journal of Social Work Education, 59*(Suppl. 1), S36–S47. https://doi.org/10.1080/10437797.2023.2203205

Reamer, F. G. (2023). Ethical practice in a post-Roe world: A guide for social workers. *Social Work, 68*(2), 150–158. https://doi.org/10.1093/sw/swad004

Reuters. (2022, June 26). *Reactions to the supreme court overturning Roe v. Wade.* https://www.reuters.com/world/us/reactions-us-supreme-court-overturning-roe-v-wade-abortion-landmark-2022-06-24/

Romo, V. (2020, December 29). Massachusetts Senate overrides veto, passes law expanding abortion access. *NPR.* https://www.npr.org/2020/12/29/951259506/massachusetts-senate-overrides-veto-passes-law-expanding-abortion-access

Rosman, K., & Cherelus, G. (2022, June 27). Women on why they're stocking up on the morning-after pill. *The New York Times.* https://www.nytimes.com/2022/06/27/style/plan-b-stockpile-roe-abortion.html#

Smyth, J. C. (2023, November 7). Ohio voters enshrine abortion access in constitution in latest statewide win for reproductive rights. *The Associated Press.* https://apnews.com/article/ohio-abortion-amendment-election-2023-fe3e067 47b616507d8ca21ea26485270

Society for Social Work Leadership in Healthcare. (2024). *SSWLHC response to supreme court decision.* https://sswlhc.org/sswlhc-response-to-supreme-court -decision/

Swanson, K., Ravi, A., Saleh, S., Weia, B., Pleasants, E., Arvisais-Anhalt, S., & Arvisais-Anhalt, S. (2023, December). Effect of recent abortion legislation on Twitter user engagement, sentiment, and expressions of trust in clinicians and privacy of health information: Content analysis. *Journal of Medical Internet Research, 25,* e46655. https://www.jmir.org/2023/1/e46655

Ujah, O., Olaore, P., Nnorom, O., Ogbu, C., & Kirby, R. (2023, May 4). Examining ethno-racial attitudes of the public in Twitter discourses related to the United States supreme court Dobbs vs. Jackson Women's Health Organization ruling: A machine learning approach. *Frontiers in Global Women's Health, 4,* 1149441. https://pubmed.ncbi.nlm.nih.gov/37214560/

University at Buffalo School of Social Work. (2022a, July 1). *About: Statement following the Supreme Court decision overturning Roe v. Wade.* https://socialwork .buffalo.edu/about/diversity-and-social-justice/statement-supreme-court-decision -overturning-roe-v-wade.html

University at Buffalo School of Social Work. (2022b, July 12). Reproductive justice: A call to action for social work in the post-Roe world [Audio podcast episode.] In *inSocialWork.* University at Buffalo School of Social Work. https://www .insocialwork.org/reproductive-justice-a-call-to-action-for-social-work-in-the -post-roe-world/

University of Washington School of Social Work. (2024). *News & events: Joint statement on Roe v. Wade by the deans of the schools of nursing, social work, and public health.* https://socialwork.uw.edu/news/joint-statement-roe-v-wade-deans -university-washington-schools-nursing-social-work-and-public

Virginia Commonwealth University School of Social Work. (2023, February 02). *What is reproductive justice? Exploring the role of social workers.* https:// onlinesocialwork.vcu.edu/blog/what-is-reproductive-justice/

Whitesell, A. (2024, June 03). Anti-abortion rights activists navigate a new, post-Roe landscape, as state bans mean they can "save babies." *The Conversation.* https://www.yahoo.com/news/anti-abortion-rights-activists-navigate-123826379.html

Zhur, D., Zhao, L., Alzoubi, T., Shenin, N., Baskaran, T., Tikhonov, J., & Wang, C. (2024). Public health and clinical implications of Dobbs v. Jackson for patients and healthcare providers: A scoping review. *PLoS One, 19*(3), e0288947. https://pubmed.ncbi.nlm.nih.gov/38551970/

Mental Health Impacts of the Ruling

Jennifer Toof

With contributions from Erin-Lee Kelly & Mehj Aubol

The Supreme Court's decision to overturn *Roe v. Wade* in June 2022, also known as the Dobbs decision, has sparked significant discussion in the mental health community. Many experts are concerned about the psychological toll of the ruling, reinforcing the idea that barriers to abortion access can profoundly impact mental health (Anderson, 2024). Considerable research has found that people forced to carry unwanted pregnancies experience adverse financial, social, physical, and mental health effects (Herd et al., 2016; Tobón et al., 2023). These negative effects may be more severe for survivors of domestic abuse/ intimate partner violence, survivors of rape/incest, or people in marginalized groups, such as persons living in poverty, people of color, and members of the LGBTQ+ community (Abrams, 2023a; Ogbu-Nwobodo, 2022). Moreover, research increasingly shows that the negative effects of the new legal restrictions go beyond those directly denied an abortion and affect the broader population, particularly women of reproductive age (Steinberg, 2024; Thornburg, 2024). This chapter provides an overview of relevant research in this area. Additionally, personal narratives from mental health professionals, clients, and others impacted by the ruling are shared to illustrate the lived experiences behind the data.

Mental Health Effects of Having an Abortion

Before discussing the mental health effects of being denied an abortion, it is important to address the long-standing, inaccurate belief that having an abortion leads to negative mental health outcomes, as misinformation about abortion is linked to lower support for the procedure (Abrams, 2023b). Research from around the world has shown that although some individuals may experience negative impacts on their mental well-being as a result of having an abortion, the majority do not (Abrams, 2023b; Duszynski-Goodman, 2022). In the Turnaway Study, a landmark analysis of abortion from Advancing New Standards in Reproductive Health at the University of California, San Francisco, researchers followed nearly 1,000 women across twenty-one states for five years to examine the similarities and differences between those who wanted and received an abortion versus those who wanted but were denied an abortion (Abrams, 2023b). Five years following the procedure, those who had an abortion were not more likely to report negative emotions or suicidal ideation than those who did not have one, and over 97 percent of those studied said they felt that they made the right decision in having an abortion. The study found that some women who had an abortion in the second or third trimester due to life-threatening birth defects did experience psychological problems after the procedure but that they were comparable to the mental health problems faced by people who miscarried or who lost a newborn. Further, the distress these women reported was still less severe than that of women who did not have abortions and instead delivered babies with severe birth defects. The conclusion reached by leaders of the Turnaway Study was that abortion in and of itself does not cause mental health issues (Abrams, 2023b).

A number of studies suggesting that abortion led to posttraumatic stress disorder (PTSD), depression, or other mental health issues were found to be methodologically flawed by the American Psychological Association's Task Force on Mental Health and Abortion (Abrams, 2023b; Duszynski-Goodman, 2022). Evaluating all empirical studies conducted between 1989 and 2008, the task force concluded that the most methodologically sound research found that legally terminating an unwanted pregnancy in the first trimester did not increase the risk of negative mental health outcomes. "There is no research to indicate that abortion is a cause for subsequent mental health diagnoses," American Psychological Association president Frank C. Worrell, PhD, said in a statement separate from the report (Duszynski-Goodman, 2022, para. 9).

Mental Health Effects of Being Denied an Abortion

As detailed, despite contrary belief, there is no research to indicate that having an abortion increases one's risk for mental health problems. However, being denied an abortion and being forced to carry an unwanted pregnancy to term does increase this risk. Considerable research has found that people forced to carry unwanted pregnancies experience adverse financial, social, physical, and mental health effects.

The Turnaway Study found that women who wanted but were denied abortions experienced more anxiety and stress and lower self-esteem and life satisfaction than those who wanted and received one (Abrams, 2023b). They also experienced more economic hardships, such as worse credit scores, more frequent bankruptcies and evictions, and higher chances of living in poverty. After being denied an abortion, women were also more likely to stay with a violent partner or to raise children alone. The Turnaway Study further found that children born to people who wanted but were denied an abortion also experienced a range of social, emotional, and mental health problems that continued into adulthood. For example, these children were more likely to experience poor bonding with their mothers, live in poverty, have lowered future aspirations, and have more psychiatric hospitalizations than children of planned/wanted pregnancies (Abrams, 2023b; Clay, 2024).

Research conducted since the Turnaway Study has also found that, compared to those who had an abortion, people who were denied one report higher stress and anxiety, increased depression, lower self-esteem, lower life satisfaction, and increased risk for suicide (Abrams, 2023b; Anderson, 2024; Thornburg, 2024; Zandberg et al., 2023). The overturning of *Roe v. Wade* itself has led to anxiety, depression, resignation, hopelessness, disillusionment, and fear/concern in people across ideological lines (Abrams, 2023b). Impacts on specific populations are discussed further below.

Women of Reproductive Age

One of the groups that experts found have experienced heightened anxiety following the Dobbs decision is women of reproductive age. Mental and physical health professionals have seen clients in this group express fears that not all men will use condoms or that they may become pregnant even while using birth control and then abortion will not be available if needed. Greater anxiety surrounding sex can be damaging to intimacy. Individuals in this group have also expressed concerns about using period tracking apps and if their data could be used against them if they ever needed an abortion (Abrams, 2023b).

Case in Practice: Dr. Lee's Clients

Dr. Lee, a licensed professional counselor in Pennsylvania, noticed that the concerns voiced by female clients of reproductive age in her therapy sessions echoed the findings of the abovementioned studies. Following the Dobbs decision, Dr. Lee experienced a significant increase in women seeking therapy due to concerns about their reproductive rights. Addressing these issues has proven to be profoundly challenging for her. Many of these clients expressed deep concern about the potential loss of their right to choose abortion if legislative changes occur in their state. These fears were often accompanied by intense feelings of panic, anxiety, and hopelessness, as clients grappled with the possibility of losing autonomy over their bodies. Reflecting on the current climate, Dr. Lee observed that "Margaret Atwood's dystopian novel *The Handmaid's Tale* poignantly captures the unsettling reality many women feel when they are navigating their body autonomy," a reality Dr. Lee encounters in her therapy sessions every week. Dr. Lee's experiences in her therapy practice reflect a broader climate of fear and uncertainty among individuals navigating restrictive reproductive policies, which may have tangible and often devastating consequences.

People with Preexisting Mental Health Concerns

One of the greatest predictors of mental health after being denied an abortion is an individual's mental health prior to being denied an abortion (Abrams, 2023b). It is important to note that those seeking abortions may already have worse baseline mental health than the average person because of systemic factors that contribute to unplanned pregnancy, such as rape/incest, domestic abuse/intimate partner violence, and low socioeconomic status. Carrying an unwanted pregnancy to term may cause mental health issues for people with no prior history of mental health issues, but for a person already experiencing depression, anxiety, PTSD, or other mental health concerns, carrying an unwanted pregnancy may further exacerbate mental health issues (Arboleda, 2024; Tobón et al., 2023).

The overturning of *Roe v. Wade* could create additional barriers for people with mental health diagnoses to receive the care they need. For example, many people with significant mental health issues, such as schizophrenia, typically need psychotropic medications to stabilize their symptoms, but many of these medications are not safe for the fetus during pregnancy (Arboleda, 2024). Therefore, not being able to get an abortion could force people with significant mental health diagnoses to stop taking their medications.

Effects on Survivors of Domestic Abuse/Intimate Partner Violence

Domestic abuse/intimate partner violence is a risk factor for unplanned pregnancy, and unplanned pregnancy can lead to increased violence, creating a cycle that puts survivors at continued risk (Duszynski-Goodman, 2022). Abusive partners may refuse to use birth control or force themselves sexually on their partners. Experiencing domestic abuse/intimate partner violence is a leading reason for wanting an abortion (Tobón et al., 2023). One reason people in such situations may want an abortion is because it is easier for them to leave an abusive relationship if they are not pregnant or do not have children with the abuser. Survivors may also fear that the abusive partner may hurt the child if they go through with the pregnancy. Per Tobón et al. (2023), as many as 22 percent of those seeking abortions have been exposed to recent domestic abuse/intimate partner violence. Further, research indicates that being pregnant increases the risk of domestic abuse/intimate partner violence throughout pregnancy and for 1.5 years postpartum, with a higher share of women reporting new cases of domestic violence during pregnancy and postpartum (Duszynski-Goodman, 2022). Continued violence toward a pregnant person can be physically and mentally detrimental to the health of the pregnant person and/or fetus. The hormone cortisol is released during times of high stress, such as experiencing violence. High cortisol levels during pregnancy have been associated with premature or low birth weight (Shriyan et al., 2023). For the pregnant person, high cortisol increases the risk of developing postpartum depression and/or postpartum PTSD. (Shriyan et al., 2023) Survivors of domestic abuse/intimate partner violence in general also have higher rates of depression, anxiety, PTSD, substance abuse, and suicidal ideation (Duszynski-Goodman, 2022). Finally, pregnancy also increases one's risk of death by homicide (Duszynski-Goodman, 2022).

Effects on Survivors of Rape/Incest

Deleterious mental health effects of being denied an abortion may be exacerbated for people who become pregnant as a result of rape or incest. There is a dearth of literature on the mental health effects of rape-related pregnancy. One reason for the lack of research in this area is that, under Roe, individuals who wanted to get an abortion following rape-related pregnancy could legally do so in any American state. Another reason for the research gap is that many rape/incest survivors do not come forward and thus would not be included in a scientific study. However, it is known that rape and incest are significant risk factors for the development of PTSD and other mental health disorders. Thus, having preexisting trauma and mental health struggles on top of being forced to carry an unwanted pregnancy to term is a dangerous combination that can lead to compounded, complex trauma responses and other negative mental, physical, financial, and social impacts (Duszynski-Goodman, 2022; Tobón et al., 2023).

As previously mentioned, PTSD symptoms can become worsened when a pregnant individual is denied access to a wanted abortion. People who have been sexually assaulted often feel that someone else took control of their body and desperately seek to regain that control. Therefore, refusing abortion services for a person who has been sexually assaulted may not only exacerbate PTSD symptoms but also further reinforce the lack of control they feel over their bodies. Additionally, people who have previous experiences of sexual assault, even if the conception of the unwanted pregnancy was consensual and/or they have received trauma therapy, could still experience continued lack of control over their body if denied an abortion, thereby intensifying PTSD symptoms (Duszynski-Goodman, 2022; Tobón et al., 2023).

Case in Practice: Hadley Duvall

Hadley Duvall is an American activist who advocates for reproductive freedom and abortion rights. Born in Kentucky, she was raped and abused for years by her stepfather, eventually becoming pregnant by him at the age of twelve. Hadley miscarried and kept the pregnancy a secret for over a decade until the overturning of *Roe v. Wade*, at which time she was motivated to discuss her experience publicly. She was featured in a viral ad for Democratic Kentucky governor Andy Beshear's 2023 reelection campaign and was widely credited for helping him win. She also spoke about her experiences on stage at the 2024 Democratic National Convention and campaigned for Kamala Harris in the 2024 Presidential election, criticizing Donald Trump's remarks about abortion bans being a positive thing.

Hadley was interviewed for this book, discussing her experience becoming pregnant as a result of rape/incest and how her mental health was impacted. She also shared the issues she encountered when speaking to mental health professionals about her experiences. When Hadley became pregnant, she said she experienced significant depression. She gained weight and stopped engaging in activities she used to enjoy. Even after the miscarriage and after the abuse stopped, she struggled with her mental health. When Hadley finally mustered the courage to see a therapist, she hit additional roadblocks. A "judgmental" psychiatrist Hadley saw accused her of wanting stimulants. One therapist who she "loved" did not do telehealth when Hadley was unable to come in-person, meaning they could not continue. One therapist was "not very present"; another "talked about themselves too much." One therapist took it upon themself to tell Hadley that "some people regret abortions." Although she is actively seeking help, Hadley expressed concern that she is not getting what she, and others like her, may need, which, in her view, is compassion, empathy, and understanding delivered through a trauma-informed approach.

When *Roe v. Wade* was overturned, she described it as a "gut punch," concerned that other people who were in her situation would not have options moving forward. Kentucky, where Hadley is from, is a state where abortions are currently illegal with no exceptions for rape or incest. Had she not miscarried when she did in 2014, Hadley would have legally been able to get an abortion. Now, she would not have been able to do so and would have been forced to carry her stepfather's child to term at the age of twelve. In 2024, Hadley worked with Democratic state senator David Yates to introduce Senate Bill 99, also known as "Hadley's Law," which would have allowed for abortion exceptions in cases of rape or incest. However, the bill has yet to pass.

Effects on Marginalized Populations

Members of marginalized populations, such as people of color, members of the LGBTQ+ population, and people from lower-income backgrounds or medically underserved areas may face additional challenges and unique mental health impacts from the overturning of *Roe v. Wade*. Indeed, experts agree that these individuals will be hit the hardest by abortion bans (Abrams, 2023b). It is important to note that members of marginalized groups face more structural barriers to care to begin with. Approximately 60 percent of those seeking abortions are people of color, and approximately 50 percent live below the federal poverty line (Duszynski-Goodman, 2022). As Steinberg (2024) pointed out, people of lower socioeconomic status may experience compounded stress due to systemic inequalities in income and health care access.

Research shows that women in lower-income situations are less likely to use contraception than those who are not, resulting in a rate of unplanned pregnancy that is five times higher for women living in poverty (Duszynski-Goodman, 2022). For people already experiencing financial difficulties, the thought of having to pay for proper health care during pregnancy and the costs of giving birth, not to mention the long-term expenses of a child, can be extremely daunting. The mental health impacts of financial stressors include depression, anxiety, stress, and other negative impacts on well-being. The out-of-pocket cost to obtain an abortion is about $500 on average (Artiga et al., 2022). For people who may be struggling to pay for the cost of an abortion, traveling out of state to obtain an abortion because abortion is banned in their own state adds to the overall cost. Out-of-state travel can include price for gas or airfare, lodging, and childcare during the trip in addition to missing wages at work (Abrams, 2023b). These people may also feel forced to disclose the unwanted pregnancy to friends, family, or coworkers if they need financial assistance from these people in order to travel. Therefore, restricting access to abortions in certain states may make it impossible for some people to obtain access to an abortion (Artiga et al., 2022; Abrams, 2023b).

People of color are also likely to face significant consequences from *Roe v. Wade* being overturned (Duszynski-Goodman, 2022). Black women have historically faced generations of forced birth or forced sterilization (Coen-Sanchez et al., 2022). The overturning of *Roe v. Wade* could further reinforce the generational trauma that Black women have experienced related to lack of control over their bodies and in making medical decisions. Moreover, a study published in 2021 found that Black women would experience the greatest increase in deaths if people were denied access to abortions in the United States. Many people of color, including the majority of Black Americans, live in southern states with some of the most restrictive abortion laws. Even before the overturning of Roe, Black women's maternal mortality rates were troubling, with nearly three times the rate of deaths that white women have. Black women have much higher rates of severe maternal complications, meaning they are more likely to need life-saving abortions (e.g., in the case of ectopic pregnancy) or medications/procedures following a miscarriage that may now be illegal where they live (Duszynski-Goodman, 2022).

Members of the LGBTQ+ population must also be considered when examining disproportionate impacts of the Dobbs decision. Abortion and reproductive rights are typically discussed as in the context of straight and/or cisgender women, yet these are not the only people who get pregnant. People who identify as LGBTQ+ already experience discrimination in receiving health care, especially in regard to reproductive health care. Inequity is demonstrated through limited access to health care options, including gender-affirming services, health care providers primarily focusing on HIV/AIDS prevention and treatment, and lack of access to routine preventive screenings for issues such as cancer among this population. With regard to gender-affirming health care, there are currently efforts to limit this care even further. When medical providers fail to provide gender-affirming care, people in the LGBTQ+ community tend to avoid medical care or receive subpar care.

Case in Practice: Melissa

Melissa (name changed to protect privacy) is a white, married woman, in her late thirties. She has two teenage children with her husband. Melissa lives in Pennsylvania, where, at the time of writing, there are some restrictions on abortion but not a total ban (Guttmacher Institute, 2024). These restrictions include that pregnancy cannot be terminated after twenty-four weeks gestation and that the person must receive an abortion counseling session at least twenty-four hours before having the abortion (Guttmacher Institute, 2024).

Melissa had an abortion in the Fall of 2021, about nine months prior to the overturning of *Roe v. Wade*. When Melissa found out she was pregnant, she knew almost immediately that she wanted an abortion, even before she told her husband about the pregnancy. Upon telling her husband, he agreed that adding a third child to their family would be very financially difficult for them and was supportive of Melissa's choice. However, the abortion clinics Melissa called were booked several weeks out. Melissa did not want to wait. She said, "I just needed to get it done. Waiting would have caused me a lot of anxiety and caused me to feel more depressed than I already did." In terms of the required abortion counseling session in Pennsylvania, Melissa said, "I wanted to skip the counseling session. I didn't need it, because my mind was made up." Therefore, Melissa started looking at other options. She was able to find a telehealth provider located out of state. Melissa requested the pill option, thinking it would be less painful or invasive. Melissa was prescribed Mifeprisone and Misoprostol. Even though Melissa obtained the prescription, she ran into some unexpected roadblocks with picking up the medication. They were not able to mail the medication to her home in the state of Pennsylvania. Instead, they had her pick up the medication in Maryland.

Melissa only had to drive about two hours to obtain the medication, a much shorter drive than people in other areas may face. She did have to wait about two weeks between finding out that she was pregnant and obtaining the medication. Melissa stated:

> that couple of weeks in between felt horrible for my mental health. I felt anxious, depressed, annoyed, frustrated. I already suffer from pre-existing anxiety and depression, so having to wait for almost two weeks made my depression and anxiety so much worse. I cannot even imagine how much worse it would have been if I had to carry the pregnancy to term or even been pregnant for a longer amount of time. I kept having the fear of "what if I don't get the medication on time?"

Melissa also shared her experiences of what it was like traveling across state lines to pick up the medication she needed, expressing frustration that she was unable to obtain the medication in her home state. Melissa noted that the doctor advised her to ingest the medication while in Maryland. The doctor indicated potential repercussions of being pulled over in the car with this kind of medication. Melissa said:

> the scariest part is that the whole process made me feel like a criminal. I felt like I was engaging in a drug deal. I had to go to another state, pick up this package, and I could not cross state lines with it. I felt like I was doing something illegal or wrong when I absolutely was not. The process made me feel anxious and made me feel like I was doing something bad, when I was actually doing something that was right for me. This was healthcare for my body, but the process was making me feel ashamed of seeking the healthcare I needed.

Melissa reported how she felt immediately after ingesting the medication, saying, "after taking the medication, I immediately felt relief. This was a huge burden that had been lifted. I noticed my anxiety was decreasing immediately." Melissa also discussed the more long-term effects of having an abortion, and how the abortion impacted her mental health. Melissa stated:

> there was no sadness or mourning the loss of the fetus. I am very glad I did it. Three years later, I still have no regrets. I rarely think about it, and when I do, I just think that this was the best decision I could have made for myself and for my family at that point in my life, 100 percent. My children who were already born were my priority.

Melissa said that she anticipated her mental health would have declined not only during the pregnancy but also after childbirth. She said:

> it is a dangerous thing, forcing a person to carry a pregnancy and having a child when they do not want to or cannot. If I had that last child, I think I would have been mentally unstable. My anxiety and depression would have been negatively impacted, and I would have been unhappy. It would have added financial stressors to my family. The money that I spend on my mental health therapy would have had to be allocated to the baby instead. Having the baby meant that I would have had to choose between providing for the baby or attending to my mental health.

During the interview, Melissa shared that she also had an abortion when she was fifteen years old. She stated: "I was actually a lot more scared when I found out I was pregnant in my thirties than when I was fifteen." Melissa reported that, as a teenager, her mom was the one who encouraged her to have an abortion. She said, "I didn't really even know what abortions were or know that I had access to abortions. I was a kid." Melissa reported that terminating the pregnancy at fifteen did produce some sadness and grief, while the abortion in her thirties did not. However, Melissa reported that she was in a worse place with her mental health as a teenager. Melissa stated, "I remember thinking that I wanted someone to just love me and that maybe the child would love me. Now I'm thinking that if I would have had that child, my mental health would have been much worse over the years. The thought of me being pregnant at 15 is now really scary."

Melissa discussed her experiences with having an abortion at age fifteen and what the process was like for her at that time. Melissa reported going into an abortion clinic in Pennsylvania and encountering protestors outside of the abortion clinic. She said, "there were protestors outside calling me a murderer. I felt a lot of shame having that abortion because of what the protestors were saying to me." In Pennsylvania, there are no laws prohibiting protestors outside of an abortion clinic (Guttmacher Institute, 2024). Melissa reported that the medical providers at the abortion clinic treated her with respect and kindness and explained everything to her in a helpful manner. However, her interactions with the protestors negatively impacted her mental health. Melissa said, "for a long time, I thought that I was an awful person because of what the protestors said to me." Melissa's previous experience of having an in-person, surgical abortion led her to avoid an in-person appointment with her second abortion. Now, not only are there restrictions on in-person, surgical abortion procedures in many states, but nonsurgical/medication abortions and other prescription medications related to pregnancy could be severely restricted.

Case in Practice: Candance

Candance, a nineteen-year-old woman of color, decided to see a mental health professional when she was fourteen weeks pregnant. Candance lived in a state where abortion was banned except for cases of rape or incest. She experienced suicidal thoughts since she found out she was pregnant. She reported that her relationship was physically, emotionally, and financially abusive, and that she does not feel that she is mentally prepared to bring a child into the world. "This is my worst nightmare . . . that I would be forced to carry a child that would be susceptible to never ending poverty and potential abuse in the home." Candance said she was consumed with thoughts about ending her life because she did not believe that she was totally prepared to leave her abusive partner and feared that he would continue to harm her and eventually harm their child. She reported having no familial support and that her two minimum-wage jobs would not allow her to sufficiently raise a child without government assistance. Candance said she felt she was left with only one choice, and that was to end her life to avoid feeling the responsibility for bringing a child into her toxic world.

Candance's story highlights her desire for control over her life. The decision to either terminate her pregnancy or end her relationship feels like a crucial turning point for her. Her yearning to escape from the abuse and oppression she faces manifests as a desire to escape life itself. As Steinberg (2024) highlighted, people of color and those in lower-income brackets are disproportionately affected by restrictive abortion laws, with limited access to health care and fewer resources to navigate unwanted pregnancies. Candance's story provides a personal lens into these systemic issues, underscoring how the lack of options amplifies feelings of hopelessness and desperation. Her experience reflects the urgent need to address both the fundamental barriers and the mental health crises that restrictive reproductive policies exacerbate, particularly for the most vulnerable populations.

Case in Practice: Kelsie and Kyleigh

Two cases in Texas further illustrate the negative outcomes of restrictive reproductive care. In 2024, the Center for Reproductive Rights filed complaints against two Texas hospitals for refusing to treat two women, Kelsie Norris-De La Cruz and Kyleigh Thurman, with life-threatening ectopic pregnancies. Kelsie Norris-De La Cruz, from the Dallas-Fort Worth area, began cramping and bleeding soon after learning she was pregnant. Despite her worsening symptoms, the hospital staff dismissed her, labeling her condition as a miscarriage, and refused treatment. Desperate, Kelsie contacted other clinics but was told that hospitals across Texas were delaying care for ectopic pregnancies. Finally, a friend's OB-GYN reviewed her ultrasound and performed emergency surgery, but, by then, Kelsie had lost most of her right fallopian tube, affecting her future fertility. She believes the hospital's refusal to help put her life in serious danger, saying that "the doctors knew I needed an abortion, but these bans are making it nearly impossible to get basic emergency healthcare" (Center for Reproductive Rights, 2024, para. 9).

Similarly, Kyleigh Thurman from Burnet, Texas, struggled to get treatment for her ectopic pregnancy. Although her OB-GYN urged the hospital to give her a critical injection, staff turned her away multiple times. Her OB-GYN eventually had to visit the hospital in person to advocate for her, and they finally administered the necessary injection, but it came too late. Kyleigh suffered a ruptured ectopic pregnancy that required surgery, removing her right fallopian tube and affecting her fertility. On filing the complaint against the hospital, Kyleigh said:

> I never imagined I would find myself in the crosshairs of my home state's extreme abortion bans. For weeks, I was in and out of emergency rooms trying to get the abortion that I needed to save my future fertility and life. This should have been an open and shut case. Yet, I was left completely in the

dark without any information or options for the care I deserved. Pregnancy is not straightforward, and I now must live with the consequences of these extreme laws every day. None of this should have happened to me, and I want to make sure this doesn't happen to anyone else. (Center for Reproductive Rights, 2024, para 12)

Cases like Kelsie's and Kyleigh's highlight how policies limiting abortion access extend beyond emotional distress, posing significant threats to physical health and safety. The reluctance of Texas hospitals to provide timely care for life-threatening conditions such as ectopic pregnancies underscore the systemic barriers people face in accessing essential medical treatment. This confluence of psychological and physical harm reveals the far-reaching impacts of restrictive reproductive laws.

If Kyleigh or Kelsie had sought out mental health treatment for concerns regarding their limited access to reproductive health care, the mental health professionals would be tasked with managing the complexities of preventable diagnosis of infertility. People who have experienced this type of trauma may develop major depressive symptoms, such as sadness, hopelessness, loss of interest or lack of pleasure in life activities, irritability, fatigue, memory loss, sleep disturbances, and reduced or increased appetite and weight. Literature consistently shows that infertility is associated with increased rates of depression and anxiety. Bagade et al. (2022) conducted a longitudinal study that found women experiencing infertility reported higher odds of self-reported depression compared to those without infertility. Specifically, out of 5,936 women surveyed, 1,031 with infertility exhibited significantly greater psychological distress, reinforcing the notion that infertility adversely affects mental health (Bagade et al., 2022). This aligns with findings by Mir et al. (2020) showing that infertile women experience higher levels of anxiety and depression compared to their fertile counterparts, exacerbated by relationship dynamics and feelings of isolation.

Abortion Restrictions and Suicide

Zandberg et al. (2023) observed that states with more restrictive abortion laws saw higher suicide rates among women of reproductive age. The issue of suicide rates among pregnant individuals is a critical area of research, as it highlights the mental health challenges faced during pregnancy. Research indicates that pregnant individuals are at an increased risk for suicidal behaviors compared to the general population. For instance, a study by Kitsantas et al. (2020) found that the prevalence of suicidal behaviors during pregnancy was approximately 3.4 percent, which aligns with previous research suggesting that pregnant people experience higher rates of suicidal ideation than nonpregnant people. Similarly, a systematic review by Gelaye et al. (2016) noted that while maternal deaths from obstetric causes have decreased, the rates of maternal deaths attributable to suicide have remained stable.

Various studies have documented the prevalence of suicidal ideation and behaviors in this population, revealing significant variations across different regions and demographics. In specific populations of pregnant people, the rates of suicidal ideation are even greater. For example, a study conducted in Brazil, where abortion is a crime punishable by a year or more in prison, reported that 18.4 percent of pregnant women exhibited current suicide risk (Abdelghani et al., 2019). In contrast, some research suggests that pregnancy may serve as a protective factor against suicidal behavior in certain contexts. Trettim et al. (2020) found that while pregnant women with a history of suicide attempts reported current suicidal ideation, the overall incidence of suicidal behavior was minimal in their sample, indicating a potential protective effect of pregnancy. This contrasts with findings from other studies that emphasize the vulnerability of pregnant individuals to mental health issues, including depression and anxiety, which are significant risk factors for suicidal ideation (Castro e Couto et al., 2015; Legazpi et al., 2022).

The literature reveals a concerning prevalence of suicidal ideation and behaviors among pregnant individuals, with significant variations based on geographic and socioeconomic factors. While some studies suggest a protective effect of pregnancy, the overall risk remains substantial, necessitating targeted mental health interventions and support systems to mitigate these risks. This research highlights the need for further studies to fully understand the individual-level mental health effects of policies such as abortion bans that could increase suicide risk among pregnant individuals.

Abortion Stigma

The stigma surrounding abortion must be considered when discussing mental health. People who consider but are denied access to abortion may feel isolated and ashamed, further worsening their mental health. Banning the procedure also stigmatizes it, and stigma harms mental health, according to findings from the Turnaway Study. Women in the study who felt they would be looked down on by friends, family, and community members if they had an abortion were much more likely to report psychological distress years later (Abrams, 2023b).

Conclusion

Considerable research paired with stories from professionals and individuals paint a stark picture of the current reality for Americans in a post-Roe world. The ongoing discussion surrounding the mental health effects of the Dobbs decision is crucial. As we continue to understand the impact of these restrictions, it is essential for researchers, policymakers, and health care providers to address the mental health needs of people who may be impacted, particularly those from vulnerable populations who are most affected by restrictive laws. The conversation around reproductive rights must consider the various mental health consequences of abortion laws.

Discussion Questions

1) What other mental health impacts do you think could arise from being denied an abortion?
2) How do you think being forced to carry an unwanted pregnancy may cause a psychological burden for the whole family, not just the pregnant individual?
3) How do you think the overturning of *Roe v. Wade* could impact the existing mental health crisis in the United States?

4) What other groups of people may be disproportionately affected by the overturning of *Roe v. Wade*?

5) How do you think abortion stigma impacts a client's willingness to talk about abortion in the counseling session?

6) In your professional work, how can you support the mental well-being of clients/patients from diverse groups who may be experiencing negative effects of abortion restrictions?

References

Abdelghani, M., Youssef, U., Sleem, N., & Hanafy, R. (2019). Prevalence and associated factors of suicide among pregnant women at Zagazig University hospitals. *Zagazig University Medical Journal, 25*(2), 216–226. https://doi.org/10.21608/zumj.2019.26922

Abrams, Z. (2023a, June 1). Abortion bans cause outsized harm for people of color. *Monitor on Psychology, 54*(4). https://www.apa.org/monitor/2023/06/abortion-bans-harm-people-of-color

Abrams, Z. (2023b, April 21). The facts about abortion and mental health. *Monitor on Psychology, 53*(6). https://www.apa.org/monitor/2022/09/news-facts-abortion-mental-health

Anderson, J. (2024). Mental health implications of abortion restrictions: A national study. *Journal of Public Health, 45*(2), 123–135.

Arboleda, N. N. (2024). Mental health implications of abortion and abortion restriction: A brief narrative review of U.S. longitudinal studies. *American Journal of Psychiatry Residents' Journal, 20*(1), 11–15. DOI: 10.1176/appi.ajp-rj.2024.200106

Artiga, S., Rudowitz, R., & Lawton, E. (2022, July 15). *What are the implications of the overturning of roe v. wade for racial disparities?* Kaiser Family Foundation Issue Brief. Kaiser Family Foundation.

Bagade, T., Thapaliya, K., Breuer, E., Kamath, R., Li, Z., Sullivan, E., & Majeed, T. (2022). Investigating the association between infertility and psychological distress using Australian longitudinal study on women's health (ALSWH). *Scientific Reports, 12*(1). https://doi.org/10.1038/s41598-022-15064-2

Castro e Couto, T., Brancaglion, M. Y. M., Cardoso, M. N., Faria, G. C., Garcia, F. D., Nicolato, R., Aguiar, R. A. L. P., Leite, H. V., & Corrêa, H. (2015). Suicidality among pregnant women in Brazil: Prevalence and risk factors. *Archives of Women's Mental Health, 19*(2), 343–348. https://doi.org/10.1007/s00737-015-0552-x

Center for Reproductive Rights. (2024, August 12). *Center files complaints against Texas hospitals for denying women emergency care for life-threatening ectopic pregnancies.* https://reproductiverights.org/texas-emtala-complaints-ectopic -pregnancies/

Clay, R. A. (2024, January 1). Policymakers are taking aim at women and LGBTQ+ individuals. *Monitor on Psychology, 55*(1). https://www.apa.org/monitor/2024/01/ trends-policy-developments-women-lgbtq

Coen-Sanchez, K., Idriss-Wheeler, D., Bancroft, X., Lau, M., Amir, S., & Medaglia, L. (2022). Reproductive justice in patient care: Tackling systemic racism and health inequities in sexual and reproductive health and rights in Canada. *Reproductive Health, 19*(1), 44. https://doi.org/10.1186/s12978-022-01328-7

Duszynski-Goodman, L. (2022, June 24). Roe v. Wade has been overturned: How the future of abortion care in the U.S. may impact mental health, according to experts. *Forbes.* https://www.forbes.com/health/mind/roe-v-wade-mental-health/

Gelaye, B., Kajeepeta, S., & Williams, M. (2016). Suicidal ideation in pregnancy: An epidemiologic review. *Archives of Women's Mental Health, 19*(5), 741–751. https:// doi.org/10.1007/s00737-016-0646-0

Guttmacher Institute. (2024). *Abortion policies in Pennsylvania.* https://states .guttmacher.org/policies/pennsylvania/abortion-policies

Herd, P., Higgins, J., Sicinski, K., & Merkurieva, I. (2016). The implications of unintended pregnancies for mental health in later life. *American Journal of Public Health, 106*(3), 421–429. https://doi.org/10.2105/AJPH.2015.302973

Kitsantas, P., Aljoudi, S., Adams, A., & Booth, E. (2020). Prevalence and correlates of suicidal behaviors during pregnancy: Evidence from the national survey on drug use and health. *Archives of Women's Mental Health, 24*(3), 473–481. https://doi.org /10.1007/s00737-020-01089-x

Legazpi, P., Rodríguez-Muñoz, M., Olivares-Crespo, M., & Izquierdo-Méndez, N. (2022). Review of suicidal ideation during pregnancy: Risk factors, prevalence, assessment instruments, and consequences. *Psicologia Reflexão E Crítica, 35*(1). https://doi.org/10.1186/s41155-022-00220-4

Mir, R., Zahid, S., & Ehsan, S. (2020). Effect of relationship dynamics and isolation on mental health of infertile women. *Khyber Medical University Journal.* https://doi .org/10.35845/kmuj.2020.19655

Ogbu-Nwobodo, L., Shim, R. S., Vinson, S. Y., Fitelson, E. M., Biggs, M. A., McLemore, M. R., Thomas, M., Godzich, M., & Mangurian, C. (2022). Mental health implications of abortion restrictions for historically marginalized populations. *The New England Journal of Medicine, 387*(17), 1613–1617. https://doi.org/10.1056/NEJMms2211124

Shriyan, P., Sudhir., P., van Schayck., O. C. P., & Babu, G. R. (2023). Association of high cortisol levels in pregnancy and altered fetal growth. Results from the MAASTHI, a prospective cohort study, Bengaluru. *The Lancet Regional Health – Southeast Asia, 14.* https://doi.org/10.1016/j.lansea.2023.100196

Steinberg, J. (2024). The intersection of reproductive rights and mental health: Understanding post-Dobbs outcomes. *Health Equity, 56*(3), 197–210.

Thornburg, C. (2024). Anxiety and depression in women denied abortion services: A longitudinal study. *Journal of Clinical Psychology, 80*(1), 33–45.

Tobón, A. L., McNicholas, E., Clare C. A., Ireland, L. D., Payne, J. L., Moore Simas, T. A., Scott, R. K., Becker M., & Byatt, N. (2023). The end of Roe v. Wade: Implications for women's mental health and care. *Frontiers in Psychiatry, 14,* 1087045. https://doi.org/10.3389/fpsyt.2023.1087045

Trettim, J. P., de Matos, M. B., da Cunha, G. K., Martins, C. R. de S., Rubin, B. B., Scholl, C. C., de Mello, D. B., Ardais, A. P., Motta, J. V. dos S., Nedel, F., Ghisleni, G. C., Pinheiro, K. A. T., Pinheiro, R. T., & Quevedo, L. de A. (2020). Pregnancy as protection for suicidal behavior: A population-based study in south Brazil. *Revista Eletrônica Acervo Saúde, 12*(1), e2083. https://doi.org/10.25248/reas.e2083.2020

Zandberg, J., Waller, R., Visoki, E., & Barzilay, R. (2023). Association between state-level access to reproductive care and suicide rates among women of reproductive age in the United States. *JAMA Psychiatry, 80*(2), 127–134. https://doi.org/10.1001/jamapsychiatry.2022.4394

Professional Ethics Codes

Ami Crowley

Ethical codes and guidelines have been developed by various mental health associations for the purpose of setting professional standards for appropriate behavior, defining professional expectations, and preventing harm to clients. Mental health professionals have an obligation to be familiar with their professional code of ethics and its application to their professional services. All behavioral health professions agree to abide by codes of ethical practice specific to their disciplines, including, but not limited to, social workers, professional counselors, psychologists, marriage and family counselors, and mental health counselors.

As we consider the potential implications of the changes in our country regarding reproductive rights, there are many ethical considerations to be made. The overturning of *Roe v. Wade* (the US Supreme Court decision that legalized abortion nationwide in 1973) in 2022 has significant ethical, legal, and social implications, all of which counselors must be aware of when working with clients regardless of the client's gender and current status of reproduction.

The most immediate ethical implication involves the infringement on individual autonomy, particularly the right of women and pregnant people to make decisions about their own bodies. Ethical theories of autonomy argue that individuals should have the freedom to make choices about their own health, including whether or not to continue a pregnancy (Thomson, 1971). With the overturning of *Roe v. Wade*, many states have enacted or are planning to enact stricter abortion laws, which could force individuals to carry unwanted pregnancies to term or travel out of state to seek an abortion. This can lead to ethical dilemmas around bodily integrity and the right to self-determination (Greenhouse & Siegel, 2011).

The ruling disproportionately affects marginalized groups, including people of color, low-income individuals, and those in rural areas who may have less access to health care, including abortion services. Restrictions on abortion may deepen existing social inequities, as wealthier individuals can afford to travel or seek private care, while marginalized communities may face greater barriers to reproductive health care. This creates ethical concerns about fairness, justice, and equality under the law (Sanger, 2022).

The decision raises questions about the role of government in regulating personal health choices. Critics argue that government intervention in reproductive health can be seen as a violation of the separation of church and state, especially since some opposition to abortion is rooted in religious beliefs. The involvement of religious ideology in legal decisions about reproductive rights raises concerns about the ethics of imposing one particular moral or religious viewpoint on a diverse population. It can also be seen as a form of coercion, where religious beliefs override personal autonomy (Cohen, 2020).

Restricting access to legal abortions may drive people to seek unsafe, illegal abortions, which could have serious health consequences (Foster et al., 2018). Ethical considerations around public health argue that access to safe and legal abortion is critical for protecting individuals' health. Limiting access may result in increased morbidity and mortality from unsafe abortion procedures, putting women's lives at risk (WHO, 2015).

One of the central debates in the abortion controversy is the moral status of the fetus. Anti-abortion advocates argue that the fetus has a right to life, which they believe should be protected from conception, while pro-choice advocates argue that the rights of the pregnant person outweigh the rights of the fetus in the early stages of pregnancy. The decision to grant legal personhood to a fetus raises difficult ethical questions about when life begins and how to balance competing moral interests—those of the fetus and those of the pregnant person. There is no clear consensus on the ethical status of the fetus, which complicates the ethical considerations in the debate (Marquis, 1989).

The restriction or outright banning of abortion is likely to lead to unsafe, illegal abortions, particularly in states with stringent abortion laws. Studies show that restricting access to legal abortion increases the risks of maternal mortality and morbidity, as individuals may seek unsafe procedures. From an ethical perspective, the state has a responsibility to protect the health and well-being of its citizens. Limiting access to abortion increases the likelihood of dangerous, unsafe procedures, which can harm individuals' physical and mental health, raising serious public health concerns (Foster et al., 2018).

Forcing individuals to carry an unwanted pregnancy to term could have significant psychological and emotional consequences, including increased levels of stress, anxiety, and depression (Lepore & Ho, 2018). The ethics of mental health and well-being are invoked when discussing the potential long-term harm of being denied an abortion. Forcing someone to continue a pregnancy against their will could lead to detrimental effects on their mental health, which should be considered when making decisions that impact individuals' lives.

The decision could also affect family dynamics, especially when considering situations of financial instability, abusive relationships, or cases where a pregnancy is the result of rape or incest (Baker & Hoh, 2019; Shah et al., 2011). In these cases, the ethical question revolves around whether individuals should be compelled to bear children in circumstances that could lead to further trauma or hardship. The decision may also have long-term effects on the children born under such conditions, raising questions about the ethics of ensuring a stable, supportive environment for children (Rocca et al., 2015).

The overturning of *Roe v. Wade* raises fears that the Supreme Court could be setting a precedent for overturning other key privacy rights, such as access to contraception, same-sex marriage, or gender-affirming health care. This raises ethical concerns about the potential erosion of other fundamental rights and freedoms (Stone, 2022). The ruling suggests that rights not explicitly stated in the Constitution, such as the right to privacy, may be subject to reversal. This could have a broader impact on other civil rights and liberties that are deeply embedded in US constitutional law.

The ruling reflects a shift in power from federal oversight to state-level regulation of abortion laws. Some argue that this could lead to inconsistencies in access to health care across the country (Greenhouse & Siegel, 2011; Siegel, 2022). Ethical concerns about the role of the state in regulating reproductive rights arise, particularly when the rights of individuals in one state can be very different from those in another, creating a patchwork of rights and access.

In summary, overturning *Roe v. Wade* brings a range of ethical issues to the forefront, from questions of autonomy and equality to the implications for public health, mental well-being, and the broader impact on social justice. These issues involve balancing the rights of the individual with competing moral and political considerations about the rights of a fetus and the role of government in personal health care decisions.

Integrity of the Counselor

Safeguarding the integrity of the counselor is an important ethical standard for several key reasons. The relationship between a counselor and a client is built on trust. Clients rely on counselors for guidance, support, and a safe space to work through personal issues. If a counselor's integrity is compromised—through unethical behavior, dishonesty, or lack of professionalism—it can damage this trust. Once trust is lost, the effectiveness of counseling is significantly undermined. A counselor's ethical behavior is foundational to their credibility and the therapeutic process.

Counselors hold significant power and responsibility when it comes to guiding their clients. If counselors act with integrity, they provide a safe, ethical, and transparent environment for clients. A breach in integrity—such as conflicts of interest, dishonesty, or personal misconduct—can lead to harm, including emotional distress or exploitation. Counselors have an ethical duty to protect the well-being of their clients by maintaining personal and professional integrity.

The profession of counseling has established ethical codes (such as those provided by the American Counseling Association [ACA], the American Psychological Association [APA], etc.) to ensure that counselors uphold high standards of conduct. These standards are designed to protect both clients and the profession itself. Counselors who maintain their integrity serve as role models, demonstrating ethical behavior and ensuring that counseling remains a respected and trusted field.

Counselors must maintain a clear boundary between personal interests and professional responsibilities. Safeguarding their integrity includes avoiding conflicts of interest that might influence their judgment, such as having personal relationships with clients or accepting gifts. Failure to do so can lead to biased or unfair treatment of clients, which can compromise the counseling process.

Counselors frequently encounter complex ethical dilemmas in their practice. The integrity of the counselor helps ensure that decisions are made based on professional ethics rather than personal biases, external pressures, or selfish motivations. By adhering to ethical standards, counselors are more likely to make decisions that prioritize the needs and best interests of the client.

When counselors fail to act with integrity, it affects the entire field. The public's perception of counseling and therapy can be negatively influenced by the actions of a few individuals who breach ethical standards. By safeguarding their integrity, counselors contribute to the continued respect and recognition of the profession.

Counselor integrity is crucial when supporting reproductive rights as it ensures that individuals are empowered to make informed, independent decisions about their own bodies and futures. A counselor must provide unbiased information, acknowledging the individuals' values, preferences, and circumstances, rather than imposing their own beliefs. This is a highly personal, emotional, and sometimes difficult decision-making process. Trusting the counselor with sensitive information is key, and integrity ensures that confidentiality is respected. This trust allows for open dialogue, helping individuals navigate their feelings and options. This also means providing compassionate and empathetic support. A counselor must offer emotional guidance without judgment, ensuring all individuals feel heard and supported in their decision-making process, regardless of the choices they make. Counselors should never coerce or manipulate individuals into a particular decision. Integrity requires counselors to present all available options in a neutral, factual manner, allowing the individual to make their choice based on their personal situation, values, and health needs. Counselors have an ethical obligation to provide care that aligns with the best interests of the client. Acting with integrity ensures that the counseling is rooted in professional ethics, which prioritize the well-being and autonomy of the individual seeking support.

The Counseling Relationship

The counseling relationship is an important ethical standard for several key reasons, as it is foundational to the therapeutic process and the well-being of the client. The counseling relationship is built on trust, which is essential for clients to feel safe enough to explore their personal challenges, emotions, and vulnerabilities. Clients often come to counseling in times of distress and may share deeply personal information. Ethical counselors create a safe, nonjudgmental space where clients can be open and honest without fear of being exploited or harmed. Trust is fundamental to effective therapy and cannot be established without a strong, ethical counselor–client relationship.

An ethical counseling relationship is one where the counselor respects the client's autonomy, values, and personal choices. This means that the counselor does not impose their own beliefs or values on the client but instead supports the client in making their own decisions and finding their own path to healing. It is crucial that the counselor maintains an ethical standard of respecting the client's autonomy while also providing guidance and support.

One of the cornerstones of the counseling relationship is confidentiality. Ethical counselors are committed to protecting the privacy of their clients and are transparent about the limits of confidentiality. This includes explaining circumstances where confidentiality might be broken (such as in cases of harm to self or others). The assurance of confidentiality allows clients to speak freely and openly, knowing their information will not be shared without their consent, except in specific, ethically justified situations.

Maintaining clear and appropriate boundaries is essential in the counseling relationship to avoid conflicts of interest, exploitation, or harm. Ethical standards require counselors to establish and maintain professional boundaries, ensuring that the relationship remains focused on the client's well-being and growth. This includes avoiding any form of dual relationships (e.g., counselor–

client friendships or romantic relationships) that could create conflicts of interest or compromise the objectivity and integrity of the counseling process.

In the counseling relationship, the counselor holds a position of power and influence, which requires careful ethical management. The counselor must be mindful of the potential for misuse of power and should strive to empower the client, rather than control or dominate the relationship. Ethical counselors seek to support clients in becoming more self-aware and self-reliant, helping them to make informed choices and take responsibility for their own healing.

The counseling relationship is centered on the needs of the client, and the counselor's primary ethical responsibility is to act in the best interest of the client. The counselor must focus on the client's needs, concerns, and goals, without allowing personal biases or agendas to influence the therapeutic process. The ethical counselor is committed to putting the client's well-being first, offering empathy, understanding, and support in a nonjudgmental manner.

An essential aspect of the counseling relationship is the commitment to preventing harm. Counselors must be vigilant about ensuring that their actions and words do not cause emotional, psychological, or physical harm to clients. They must also be aware of potential vulnerabilities in clients and take steps to avoid exploitation or manipulation. Ethical standards help guide counselors in creating a safe and supportive environment, where clients are treated with respect and dignity.

An ethical counseling relationship requires counselors to be culturally sensitive and inclusive, recognizing and respecting the diverse backgrounds, values, and identities of their clients. Counselors must be aware of how cultural differences may impact the counseling process and adjust their approaches accordingly to ensure that all clients are treated fairly and equitably.

The counseling relationship also sets expectations for professionalism and accountability. Ethical counselors are responsible for their actions, remain self-aware, and are open to feedback. By adhering to ethical guidelines and maintaining professionalism in their relationships with clients, counselors uphold the standards of their profession and contribute to its integrity and trustworthiness.

The counseling relationship is vital when supporting reproductive rights because it creates a safe, supportive, and empowering environment where individuals can make informed decisions about their reproductive health. Reproductive decisions are deeply personal and can be emotionally charged. A strong counseling relationship fosters trust, where individuals feel safe to discuss sensitive topics without fear of judgment. Confidentiality is essential, as individuals need assurance that their private information will be protected, enabling open and honest conversations about their options and experiences. The counseling relationship can help individuals feel empowered to make informed decisions about their reproductive health. This approach respects the individual's autonomy, supporting them to make decisions that align with their values, beliefs, and life circumstances. Reproductive decisions, especially those involving abortion or unintended pregnancies, can be emotionally complex and overwhelming. A strong counseling relationship provides emotional support, helping individuals process their feelings, cope with stress, and navigate the emotional challenges that may arise during their decision-making process. The counselor's role is to listen, validate emotions, and offer compassion without judgment. For many, reproductive health choices, especially abortion, may be associated with stigma or fear of judgment from others. A trusted counseling relationship can help reduce these feelings of shame or isolation by providing a nonjudgmental, supportive space. Counselors are responsible for providing accurate, evidence-based information about reproductive health options. In a counseling relationship, clients have the opportunity to ask questions, clarify doubts, and explore the risks and benefits of each option available to them. This empowers individuals to make decisions based on comprehensive, factual information rather than misinformation or pressure from others. Counselors who understand the importance of reproductive rights can play a crucial role in advocating for their clients, ensuring they are aware of their legal rights and health care options. This advocacy helps individuals navigate legal, social, and medical barriers to accessing reproductive health care, which is especially important in regions where reproductive rights may be restricted or under threat. Counselors help individuals build resilience by developing coping strategies to manage difficult emotions or challenges related to reproductive decisions. This support strengthens the individual's ability to handle external pressures and internal conflicts, ensuring they feel more confident and prepared in their decision-making process.

Do No Harm

Nonmaleficence, which translates to "do no harm," is a critical ethical standard in counseling for several important reasons. It is a core principle in ensuring that the counseling process is safe, supportive, and beneficial for the client. The primary goal of counseling is to support clients in addressing their issues, improving their mental health, and enhancing their well-being. Counselors are in a position of trust and power, and their actions have the potential to cause both positive and negative effects on clients. By adhering to the principle of nonmaleficence, counselors are committed to avoiding actions that might harm clients, whether through inappropriate interventions, harmful advice, or exploitation. This ensures the safety and psychological integrity of the client throughout the therapeutic process.

Counseling involves exploring sensitive, often painful emotions, past trauma, and personal vulnerabilities. Without a commitment to nonmaleficence, there is a risk that these vulnerable states could be mishandled, leading to psychological harm such as emotional distress, retraumatization, or exacerbation of existing mental health conditions. Counselors are responsible for ensuring that they approach clients with care and sensitivity, creating a supportive environment that minimizes the risk of harm.

Counselors often face complex ethical dilemmas during therapy. Nonmaleficence guides counselors in making decisions that prioritize the safety and well-being of clients. It serves as a safeguard against decisions that could inadvertently harm clients or lead to negative outcomes. For example, if a counselor is uncertain about the effectiveness of a particular approach, the principle of nonmaleficence may lead them to err on the side of caution and seek alternative strategies, rather than pursuing an approach that could cause harm.

Counselors must always be aware of the inherent power imbalance in the counselor–client relationship. Without nonmaleficence, there is a risk that counselors could exploit this power—whether emotionally, financially, or even inappropriately—using the client's vulnerabilities for personal gain. Nonmaleficence ensures that counselors uphold professional boundaries and maintain an ethical stance in their relationships, preventing any form of exploitation.

Nonmaleficence is closely tied to beneficence, the ethical principle of "doing good" or promoting the welfare of others. While beneficence encourages counselors to take actions that benefit clients, nonmaleficence ensures that those actions do not inadvertently cause harm. It sets the necessary limits on actions by focusing on the importance of minimizing negative consequences. Both principles are essential for achieving positive therapeutic outcomes without compromising the client's safety or well-being.

The ethical standard of nonmaleficence upholds the integrity of the counseling profession by ensuring that counselors do not engage in practices or behaviors that could harm the public perception of counseling. For instance, counselors who act without consideration of harm may be subject to professional misconduct, legal consequences, and damage to the reputation of the field. By adhering to this principle, counselors maintain professional trust and credibility (ACA, 2014, A.4.a.; APA, 2017, 3.04).

Counselors work with individuals from diverse backgrounds, including those who may be particularly vulnerable—such as children, those experiencing trauma, people with mental health issues, or individuals facing significant life stressors. Nonmaleficence is especially crucial when working with these populations, as they may be more susceptible to harm if not treated with careful attention and ethical consideration. Protecting them from harm is a key aspect of ethical counseling practice.

By following the principle of nonmaleficence, counselors are encouraged to engage in continuous self-reflection, professional development, and supervision to maintain competence. This helps counselors avoid making harmful or ill-informed decisions that could negatively impact clients. For example, a counselor who recognizes the limits of their expertise or knowledge in a particular area may refer a client to a more experienced professional to ensure the client's well-being is not jeopardized.

Counselors' commitment to "do no harm" means that those presenting concerns related to reproductive health will not be subject to the imposition of others' opinions about the choices they should make. By providing evidence-based and no-biased information to clients, counselors are allowing the client to make a well-informed decision regarding their bodies and their futures.

Autonomy

A counselor committed to nonmaleficence respects the autonomy of the client and avoids actions that could undermine the client's sense of control or self-worth. This includes refraining from coercion, manipulation, or any interventions that could inadvertently diminish the client's ability to make their own informed decisions. This empowerment is crucial for promoting healing and growth.

Client autonomy is crucial when supporting reproductive rights because it centers on the individual's right to make decisions about their own body and future, free from external control or coercion. At its core, client autonomy is rooted in respecting a person's fundamental right to make decisions about their own body. In reproductive health, this means acknowledging the individual's right to choose whether or not to have children, access abortion, or pursue other reproductive options. Supporting autonomy affirms that individuals have the authority to make decisions based on their values, circumstances, and beliefs. Client autonomy empowers individuals by giving them the ability to make choices that are aligned with their own needs, desires, and life goals. In reproductive health, decisions about pregnancy, abortion, or contraception are deeply personal and can affect a person's health, emotional well-being, and life trajectory.

Autonomy ensures that individuals are not forced into decisions that don't align with their values or circumstances, fostering a sense of control and self-determination. Respecting client autonomy also contributes to a person's mental and emotional well-being. When individuals feel their choices are respected and their voice is heard, they are more likely to experience a sense of confidence and emotional peace in their decision-making. When autonomy is prioritized, it reduces the stigma or judgment that may be associated with reproductive choices. Autonomy encourages a nonjudgmental approach, where individuals can seek the care and support they need without fear of condemnation. This is especially important in the context of sensitive decisions like abortion, where societal or cultural judgment can create additional stress.

In many legal systems, reproductive rights are enshrined as a matter of personal liberty and human rights. Supporting client autonomy ensures that individuals are able to exercise their legal rights fully, whether it pertains to accessing contraception, making decisions about pregnancy, or obtaining an abortion. Ethically, respecting autonomy is a foundational principle in medical and counseling practice, ensuring that decisions are made in the best interests of the individual. Client autonomy helps promote equity and social justice by ensuring that all individuals, regardless of their background or social status, have the ability to make reproductive decisions that reflect their own needs and aspirations. When autonomy is respected, people from all walks of life can access reproductive care that is equitable and tailored to their specific circumstances, helping to address disparities in access to reproductive health care.

Informed Consent

Informed consent is an essential ethical standard in counseling because it upholds the client's right to make autonomous decisions, fosters trust and transparency, prevents exploitation, and ensures that the counselor is ethically and legally accountable. By obtaining informed consent, counselors demonstrate respect for the client's dignity, protect their rights, and create a therapeutic environment where the client feels empowered and safe (ACA, 2014, A.2.a.; APA, 2017, 3.10, 10.01; AMHCA, 2020, I.B.2.; AAMFT, 2015, I.1.2.).

The informed consent process is crucial in counseling individuals on reproductive rights as a means of supporting autonomy and empowerment, respecting individual rights, avoiding coercion and manipulation, meeting legal and ethical standards, and building trust and collaboration. Overall, informed consent in reproductive rights counseling is essential for ensuring individuals can make choices that reflect their values and circumstances while safeguarding their rights, dignity, and well-being.

Imposition of Values

Counselors are aware of—and avoid imposing—their own values, attitudes, beliefs, and behaviors. Counselors respect the diversity of clients, trainees, and research participants and seek training in areas in which they are at risk of imposing their values onto clients, especially when the counselor's values are inconsistent with the client's goals or are discriminatory in nature (ACA, 2014, A.4.b.; AAMFT, 2015, I.1.1.).

It is important for counselors to avoid imposing their personal values when working with clients on reproductive rights in order to provide nonjudgmental support and cultural sensitivity. Regardless of the values, attitudes, and beliefs a counselor may hold, meeting the client where they are at and supporting them through the process is the focus of the therapeutic relationship. By refraining from imposing their own values, counselors can provide a client-centered, ethical, and effective counseling experience, which helps clients make decisions that are truly in line with their own values, beliefs, and best interests.

Confidentiality

Confidentiality is an essential ethical standard in counseling because it protects the client's privacy, fosters a safe and trusting therapeutic environment, upholds professional and legal responsibilities, and helps clients feel empowered and in control of their treatment. Without confidentiality, clients may not feel comfortable or safe enough to engage fully in the counseling process, which could undermine the effectiveness of therapy. By adhering to confidentiality principles, counselors demonstrate respect for their clients' autonomy and dignity, ensuring the highest ethical standards in their practice (ACA, 2014, B.1.c.).

Confidentiality is critically important when counseling individuals on reproductive rights to ensure building trust and safety with clients, protect the privacy of all individuals, encourage autonomy and honest communication, empower individuals to make decisions for themselves, and minimize stigma and discrimination.

Limitations of Counseling

Explaining the limitations of counseling and the counseling relationship is a fundamental ethical standard because it ensures transparency, builds trust, promotes informed consent, and manages expectations. It helps clients make informed decisions about their participation in therapy, encourages realistic views of what counseling can achieve, and fosters a safe and respectful environment. This explanation is essential for protecting both the client and the counselor and upholding the ethical integrity of the counseling profession (ACA, 2014, B.1.d.; APA, 2017, 4.02).

The limitations of counseling is an important topic to cover with individuals who are seeking support regarding reproductive rights. Individuals need to know what is and is not possible during counseling and the possible outcomes of the therapeutic process. While counselors can provide ethical and effective counseling, as with all counseling processes, there are limitations that are intended to protect all involved.

Advocacy

Advocacy work is an essential ethical responsibility for counselors because it directly supports their role in promoting client well-being, fighting for social justice, protecting clients' rights, and addressing the systemic barriers that affect mental health. By engaging in advocacy, counselors extend their ethical duty beyond individual therapy, contributing to broader societal change that can improve the lives of their clients and the community as a whole. Advocacy ensures that counselors do not simply treat symptoms but also work toward creating systemic conditions that allow all individuals to access fair, equitable, and effective care (ACA, 2014, A.7.a.; AMHCA, 2020, I.F. 2.).

Advocacy is crucial in reproductive rights for several reasons, as it helps protect individuals' access to care, education, and the ability to make informed choices about their reproductive health. Advocacy is essential in securing access to reproductive health care, including contraception, family planning services, abortion, and fertility treatments. Legal and policy changes, such as restrictions or cuts to reproductive services, can limit individuals' ability to access necessary care. Advocacy efforts help push for the protection and expansion of these services, ensuring that everyone, regardless of their socioeconomic status or geographic location, has access to the care they need. Advocacy can help raise awareness about reproductive rights, ensuring that individuals understand their options, the legal landscape, and the resources available to them. Education efforts can dispel myths and misinformation surrounding reproductive health, empower people to make informed decisions, and reduce stigma around topics such as abortion, contraception, and fertility.

Many communities, particularly marginalized groups (e.g., people of color, low-income individuals, LGBTQ+ people), face greater barriers to reproductive health care due to systemic inequalities. Advocacy is crucial in addressing these disparities, promoting policies that ensure equitable access to reproductive rights for all, and working to eliminate the discrimination and biases that affect reproductive health care access. Advocacy helps support individuals' rights to make autonomous decisions about their reproductive health. By promoting the importance of informed consent, education, and access to a range of options, advocacy empowers people to take control of their reproductive choices without fear of coercion, misinformation, or external pressure.

Advocacy is essential for pushing for legislative and policy reforms that protect reproductive rights. This includes advocating for laws that ensure access to contraception, protect abortion rights, guarantee comprehensive sex education, and support reproductive health care in underserved communities.

Without strong advocacy efforts, individuals may face increasingly restrictive laws and policies that undermine their ability to make decisions about their own bodies. Reproductive justice goes beyond the right to choose and emphasizes the need for social, economic, and political conditions that support reproductive health for all individuals. Advocacy in this context not only addresses access to services but also tackles the root causes of inequality, such as poverty, racism, and inadequate health care. It seeks to ensure that everyone has the resources and support to make decisions that are right for them and their families. Reproductive health and rights are often subjects of stigma and social taboos. Advocacy helps challenge these harmful social norms and provides a platform for people to speak openly about their reproductive health needs. This helps normalize conversations around issues like abortion, contraception, and family planning, reducing shame and ensuring that people feel supported in their decisions.

Conflict with Ethics and Laws

When counselors face a situation where ethical standards conflict with laws or legal requirements, they are often caught in a challenging position. Both ethical guidelines (such as those set by professional organizations like the ACA) and legal regulations (such as state or federal laws) are designed to protect the well-being of clients and the integrity of the counseling profession. However, there are times when these two can conflict, and counselors must navigate these situations carefully to ensure they make decisions that are in the best interest of their clients and adhere to both ethical and legal requirements.

When ethical standards and laws conflict, the welfare of the client is always a primary consideration. Counselors should assess the situation carefully, considering both the ethical implications and the legal requirements, while keeping in mind the potential risks to the client's well-being. For instance, if a legal requirement mandates the reporting of child abuse even though a counselor is ethically bound to maintain confidentiality, the counselor must report the abuse, as the safety of the client (or others) overrides confidentiality in this case.

When faced with a conflict between ethics and law, counselors should seek guidance from a supervisor, legal expert, or attorney. Counselors can consult with colleagues or supervisors who have experience in ethical and legal issues to ensure they make the most informed decision. Legal counsel can provide clarity about how laws apply in specific situations and help counselors navigate the conflict.

Ethical guidelines emphasize the importance of confidentiality, but legal exceptions (such as reporting child abuse, preventing imminent harm, or complying with a court order) exist. Counselors must educate themselves on the specific laws in their jurisdiction that affect confidentiality. Being proactive about explaining the limits of confidentiality to clients at the beginning of therapy can help manage client expectations if such situations arise.

Counselors must exercise ethical discretion when navigating situations where the law and ethics conflict. Professional integrity means adhering to the broader goals of the counseling profession, such as supporting the well-being of clients and maintaining trust in the therapeutic relationship. In some cases, this means working within the legal framework but striving to minimize harm or the negative impact of legal actions.

When counselors face conflicts between ethical standards and legal requirements, they must prioritize the welfare of their clients, follow legal guidelines, and seek consultation when necessary. They should also strive to minimize harm to clients and carefully navigate ethical dilemmas through informed decision-making, transparency, and documentation. Understanding the limitations of confidentiality, using ethical discretion, and advocating for change when appropriate helps counselors navigate these difficult situations while maintaining professional integrity and ensuring that client well-being remains at the forefront (ACA, 2014, I.1.c.; APA, 2017, 1.02).

Conflicts between counseling ethics and laws related to reproductive rights can arise in several critical areas, as counselors navigate the intersection of their professional ethical obligations and legal mandates. These conflicts are particularly significant in areas such as abortion, contraception, parental consent, and counseling minors.

Ethical counseling principles prioritize respecting the autonomy of clients in making reproductive decisions, but laws in some states restrict access to abortion or impose mandatory waiting periods, counseling, or other barriers. Some states require mandatory counseling before an abortion, which can conflict with the ethical obligation to provide unbiased, nonjudgmental support. Reproductive rights laws in many states require parental consent for minors seeking certain reproductive health services, such as contraception or abortion, while ethical guidelines emphasize the importance of maintaining confidentiality and respecting the minor's autonomy. Ethical standards require counselors to provide accurate, comprehensive information to clients about all their reproductive options. However, in some states where abortion is restricted or banned, counselors may face legal constraints in providing information or referrals related to abortion services. Counselors' personal religious beliefs about reproductive rights may conflict with their ethical duty to respect the values and choices of their clients. Laws in some states require parental notification or consent for minors seeking reproductive health services, but counselors may face an ethical dilemma in situations where the minor client's safety is at risk or when the minor seeks confidential counseling. Ethical counseling emphasizes addressing issues of reproductive justice and systemic inequalities in access to reproductive health care, but counselors may face challenges in addressing these issues due to legal restrictions or inadequate public services (ACA, 2014).

Conflicts between counseling ethics and laws regarding reproductive rights primarily arise in areas such as confidentiality, informed consent, autonomy, and mandatory reporting. Counselors must navigate these conflicts carefully, balancing their ethical obligations to respect client autonomy and confidentiality with legal mandates that may restrict or influence how they provide reproductive health services. When conflicts arise, counselors are advised to stay informed about both legal changes and ethical guidelines, seek supervision or consultation, and advocate for changes in laws that align with ethical counseling practice.

Ethical Decision-Making Models

In addition to knowing and understanding one's professional code of ethics, it is important to consider how an ethical decision is made. Ethical decision-making models are essential tools for counselors to navigate complex situations in a manner that aligns with professional ethics and guidelines. These models help counselors evaluate options, consider consequences, and make well-informed decisions that prioritize the well-being of clients. Below are several widely recognized ethical decision-making models for counselors:

The ACA provides a structured framework for counselors to follow when making ethical decisions. It emphasizes a systematic approach to considering all factors involved in the situation. The eight steps process to the ACA Ethical Decision-Making Model is as follows:

Step 1: Identify the problem or dilemma.

Step 2: Apply the ACA Code of Ethics.

Step 3: Determine the potential issues involved (e.g., legal, ethical, and cultural).

Step 4: Explore possible courses of action.

Step 5: Consider the potential consequences of each option.

Step 6: Evaluate the selected action from an ethical perspective.

Step 7: Implement the decision.

Step 8: Reflect on the decision and outcome (2014).

The 7-Step Ethical Decision-Making Model by Forester-Miller and Davis is widely used by counselors for ethical problem-solving. It helps counselors consider both the ethical implications and the professional guidelines.

Step 1: Identify the problem or dilemma.

Step 2: Identify the potential issues involved (e.g., ethical, legal, professional).

Step 3: Review the relevant ethical guidelines and professional codes.

Step 4: Know the laws and regulations that apply to the situation.

Step 5: Seek consultation with colleagues or supervisors.

Step 6: Explore alternatives and their possible consequences.

Step 7: Decide on a course of action and evaluate its ethical basis (Forester-Miller & Davis, 2016).

The Ethical Principles Screen by Koocher and Keith-Spiegel focuses on integrating ethical principles into decision-making, particularly useful when counselors face dilemmas that involve competing interests:

Step 1: Define the Problem—Understand the ethical issue.

Step 2: Consult Ethical Codes—Check the relevant ethical codes (e.g., ACA, APA, NASW, AAMFT, AMHCA).

Step 3: Consider the Consequences—Assess the potential outcomes of different actions.

Step 4: Consult With Others—Seek supervision, consultation, or peer discussion.

Step 5: Identify the Ethical Principles—Use principles such as autonomy, nonmaleficence, beneficence, justice, fidelity, and veracity to guide the decision-making process.

Step 6: Make a Decision—Choose a course of action based on the principles, consultation, and evaluation of consequences (Koocher & Keith-Spiegel, 2008).

While considered an older model, Blake's PLUS Model offers a simple and practical four-step approach to ethical decision-making by considering multiple dimensions:

Step 1: Policies—What policies, laws, or regulations apply to the situation?

Step 2: Legal—What are the legal implications of each option?

Step 3: Universal Principles—Does the decision align with universal ethical principles, such as fairness and respect for others?

Step 4: Self—Does the decision align with the counselor's personal values and professional integrity? (1964)

The Ethical Decision-Making Model of the National Association of Social Workers (NASW), though designed for social workers, is applicable to counselors as well. It encourages a thorough examination of all factors in ethical decision-making.

Step 1: Identify the ethical issue or dilemma.

Step 2: Identify the key values involved.

Step 3: Review the relevant code of ethics and legal guidelines.

Step 4: Gather all relevant facts.

Step 5: Evaluate potential courses of action and their consequences.

Step 6: Make the decision based on ethical principles.

Step 7: Implement and follow through with the decision (2017).

Corey's Integrative Ethical Decision-Making Model emphasizes understanding the client's needs and values while integrating ethical guidelines into decision-making:

Step 1: Identify the problem or dilemma.
Step 2: Identify the potential issues involved (e.g., ethical, legal, cultural).
Step 3: Review the relevant ethical codes and guidelines.
Step 4: Consult with colleagues or supervisors.
Step 5: Explore possible courses of action and their consequences.
Step 6: Make a decision based on ethical reasoning.
Step 7: Implement the decision and evaluate the outcome (Corey et al., 2015).

The Decision-Making Model of the APA guides counselors and psychologists in applying ethical principles to specific dilemmas, emphasizing systematic analysis:

Step 1: Define the problem.
Step 2: Identify possible courses of action.
Step 3: Determine the consequences of each action.
Step 4: Weigh the ethical principles and guidelines.
Step 5: Take action based on the most ethical course (2017).

In the Virtue Ethics Model by Lapsley and Narvaez, ethical decision-making is framed within the context of character and virtue. Counselors are guided by their personal and professional virtues (e.g., empathy, integrity, humility) in decision-making:

Step 1: Identify the ethical dilemma.
Step 2: Reflect on personal virtues and professional ethics.
Step 3: Consider how virtues like honesty, compassion, and respect for others influence decisions.
Step 4: Make decisions based on acting in accordance with virtuous behavior, rather than simply adhering to rules (2006).

Ethical decision-making models offer counselors structured approaches for navigating challenging dilemmas. By considering various frameworks like the ACA model, Forester-Miller and Davis's 7-step model, or the Virtue Ethics approach, counselors can make decisions that promote the well-being and dignity of their clients while adhering to professional standards.

Conclusion

Ethical codes and guidelines have been developed by various mental health associations for the purpose of setting professional standards for appropriate behavior, defining professional expectations, and preventing harm to clients. Mental health professionals have an obligation to be familiar with their professional code of ethics and its application to their professional services. All behavioral health professions agree to abide by codes of ethical practice specific to their disciplines, including, but not limited to, social workers, professional counselors, psychologists, marriage and family counselors, and mental health counselors.

Professional mental health associations have developed ethical codes and guidelines in order to establish standards of professional behavior, defining the roles of a counselor, and actively prevent harm to clients. As a mental health professional, there is an inherent obligation to not only know the ethical principles by which the practice is governed but also how to appropriately apply these principles to the professional service of counseling. When a behavioral health professional becomes licensed, they agree to abide by their professional ethical code and standards specific to their discipline, regardless of the clinical focus of their license.

Case Study

Case Study: Counseling for Abortion Consideration

Client Overview

Name: Sarah (pseudonym)
Age: Twenty-six
Occupation: Elementary school teacher

Relationship Status: In a committed relationship

Presenting Issue: Sarah is seeking counseling to explore her feelings, thoughts, and options regarding an unplanned pregnancy and the potential decision to have an abortion.

Presenting Situation

Sarah discovered she was pregnant through a home pregnancy test after missing her period for three weeks. The pregnancy was confirmed by a health care professional. This news has led to an emotional and psychological crisis, and Sarah is struggling to decide whether to continue with the pregnancy or seek an abortion.

Sarah is in a stable, long-term relationship with her partner, Michael. They are both professionals with relatively stable careers but are not married. Sarah and Michael have had ongoing discussions about their future together, but the topic of children has not been heavily explored. Michael has expressed that he feels unprepared for fatherhood at this time, and Sarah shares similar concerns about the timing and impact of a child on their personal and professional lives.

Sarah's main concerns include the following:

- Readiness for parenthood: She feels uncertain about her ability to balance the demands of being a mother with her career aspirations.
- Impact on career and finances: As a teacher, she is concerned about the financial strain that having a child could impose, particularly as her current salary is modest, and her partner is also not in a position to contribute significantly.
- Emotional readiness: Sarah questions whether she feels emotionally equipped to care for a child at this stage of her life. She is also grappling with guilt and self-doubt about the possibility of ending the pregnancy, as she has always believed in the importance of family but is unsure about her personal readiness.
- Relationship with partner: While Michael is supportive of her decision-making process, they have different perspectives on the pregnancy, with Sarah feeling that the timing is all wrong, while Michael leans toward supporting whatever choice she makes.

Therapeutic Goals

The main objectives of counseling are:

1. Clarification of values: To help Sarah explore her personal values, moral beliefs, and life goals in the context of this pregnancy.
2. Exploration of emotional and psychological impact: To provide a safe, nonjudgmental space for Sarah to process her emotions, including fear, guilt, and confusion, while exploring her deeper feelings about the potential abortion.
3. Information on options: To ensure that Sarah is fully informed of all her options, including abortion, adoption, and parenting, so she can make a decision that aligns with her values and current life circumstances.
4. Enhancing decision-making skills: To support Sarah in making an informed, autonomous decision by considering both short-term and long-term implications of each option.
5. Support with coping strategies: To help Sarah manage any emotional distress, anxiety, or conflict in her relationship with Michael as they navigate this challenging situation together.

Therapeutic Approach

The counselor utilizes a combination of person-centered therapy, cognitive-behavioral therapy (CBT), and solution-focused therapy (SFT) to address Sarah's emotional distress, confusion, and decision-making process. The counselor's approach emphasizes the following:

*   Empathy and nonjudgmental listening: Providing Sarah with a space to share her fears and concerns without feeling judged.
*   Exploring values and beliefs: Helping Sarah understand how her upbringing, cultural background, and personal beliefs might be influencing her feelings toward abortion.
*   Cognitive restructuring: Assisting Sarah in identifying any cognitive distortions, such as catastrophizing (e.g., "I'll never be able to have a

successful career if I keep this baby"), and reframing these thoughts in a more balanced and realistic manner.

- Problem-solving skills: Using SFT to focus on potential solutions and help Sarah visualize different paths forward, whether that involves parenting, adoption, or abortion, while considering the potential challenges and benefits of each.

Session 1: Initial Assessment

During the first session, Sarah discusses her fears and uncertainties about becoming a mother. The counselor listens empathetically and validates her emotional experience, allowing her to express conflicting feelings without pressure. The counselor provides a basic overview of all available options and reassures Sarah that each choice is valid and deserves careful consideration.

Sarah's anxiety is palpable as she talks about her career and financial concerns. The counselor explores these fears in more detail, and Sarah begins to recognize that a large part of her fear is based on the unknowns of motherhood rather than a fundamental lack of desire for a child.

The counselor provides resources on the practicalities of parenting, including financial assistance programs, maternity leave policies, and day care options, to help Sarah better understand the realities of raising a child in her current circumstances.

Session 2: Values Exploration

In the second session, Sarah is encouraged to reflect on her core values and life goals. The counselor uses open-ended questions to guide Sarah through an exploration of her beliefs about family, career, and motherhood.

Sarah reveals that she has always believed in having children one day but also values her independence and career progression. She acknowledges that her upbringing did not emphasize career over family, which creates a sense of conflict within her. The counselor helps Sarah recognize that her decision is deeply personal and that she can create a future that aligns with her evolving sense of self.

This session helps Sarah realize that her feelings of guilt about considering abortion are rooted in societal pressures and expectations, rather than her own desires. She begins to feel empowered to make a decision that feels right for her.

Session 3: Exploring the Impact of Abortion

In this session, the counselor gently addresses the option of abortion, acknowledging Sarah's concerns about the potential emotional fallout. Sarah expresses feelings of guilt and shame at the thought of ending the pregnancy, even though she understands that her circumstances may not support raising a child at this time.

The counselor provides factual information about the procedure, including the emotional effects of abortion, both positive and negative, and ensures that Sarah knows where to find additional support resources should she choose this path. The counselor also discusses the potential for grief, but reaffirms that Sarah's feelings are normal and valid.

At the end of this session, Sarah feels less anxious and more informed, but she is still unsure whether abortion is the right choice for her.

Session 4: Relationship Dynamics

In the fourth session, Sarah shares her concerns about her relationship with Michael. Although he is supportive of her decision, she feels some underlying tension because they have not discussed their long-term plans in detail.

The counselor facilitates a conversation about how both partners can better communicate about their respective hopes and fears. Sarah is encouraged to share her thoughts and feelings with Michael openly. The session also touches on how they can work together to make a decision that supports both of their emotional needs.

Session 5: Decision-Making

By the fifth session, Sarah has taken time to reflect on her options. She feels more clear about her priorities, which include her career aspirations, her relationship with Michael, and her desire to feel emotionally and financially stable before becoming a parent.

Sarah has learned to give herself permission to make a decision based on her current reality, rather than societal expectations or guilt. She is leaning toward seeking an abortion but wants to explore the emotional consequences of this decision further before making a final choice.

Conclusion

The counseling process has helped Sarah feel more confident in her ability to make an informed, autonomous decision. While she has not yet fully decided, she feels empowered to continue the decision-making process without the weight of guilt or shame. The counselor has provided support, information, and emotional validation, and will continue to help Sarah process her feelings as she navigates the next steps. Sarah plans to schedule an appointment with a health care provider to discuss the abortion procedure in more detail.

Follow-Up

Sarah plans to return for additional counseling sessions following her decision, to help process her emotions, whether she chooses abortion, adoption, or parenting. The counselor continues to offer support as Sarah navigates any challenges, ensuring she has a solid emotional foundation regardless of her decision.

Case Study Discussion Questions

1) What ethical standards should be considered for this case study?
2) What action steps should a counselor take after considering all the information presented in the case study?
3) What ethical decision-making model would you use and why?

References

American Association for Marriage and Family Therapy. (2015). *AAMFT code of ethics*. https://www.aamft.org/Legal_Ethics/Code_of_Ethics.aspx

American Counseling Association. (2014). *2014 ACA code of ethics*. https://www.counseling.org/resources/ethics

American Mental Health Counseling Association. (2020). *AMHCA code of ethics*. https://www.amhca.org/events/publications/ethics

American Psychological Association. (2017). *Ethical principles of psychologists and code of conduct (2002, amended effective June 1, 2010, and January 1, 2017)*. https://www.apa.org/ethics/code/

Baker, C. K., & Hoh, K. (2019). Rape, incest, and the ethics of reproductive choice. *Journal of Family Violence, 34*, 377–384.

Cohen, C. J. (2020). Religion, law, and the role of the state: A reconsideration of abortion legislation. *Journal of Political Philosophy, 28*, 379–400.

Corey, G., Corey, M. S., & Callanan, P. (2015). *Issues and ethics in the helping professions* (9th ed.). Brooks/Cole.

Forester-Miller, H., & Davis, T. E. (2016). *Practitioner's guide to ethical decision making* (Rev. ed.). http://www.counseling.org/docs/default-source/ethics/practioner's-guide-toethical-decision-making.pdf

Foster, D. G., et al. (2018). Effect of abortion restrictions on out-of-state travel for abortion in the United States. *JAMA, 320*, 2593–2600.

Greenhouse, L., & Siegel, R. B. (2011). Before (and after) Roe v. Wade: New questions about backlash. *Yale Law Journal, 120*, 211–304.

Koocher, G. P., & Keith-Spiegel, P. (2008). *Ethics in psychology and the mental health professions: Standards and cases* (2nd ed.). Oxford University Press.

Lapsley, D. K., & Narvaez, D. (2006). The four components of acting ethically: Moral sensitivity, moral judgment, moral motivation, and moral character. In M. Killen & J. Smetana (Eds.), *Handbook of moral development* (pp. 555–577). Psychology Press.

Lepore, S. J., & Ho, D. (2018). Mental health consequences of restricting abortion. *American Journal of Public Health, 108*, 635–642.

Marquis, D. (1989). Why abortion is immoral. *Journal of Philosophy, 86*, 183–202.

National Association of Social Workers. (2017). *NASW code of ethics*. https://www.socialworkers.org/About/Ethics/Code-of-Ethics/Code-of-Ethics-English

Rocca, C. H., et al. (2015). Disadvantageous effects of being denied an abortion: A longitudinal study of women who are seeking an abortion. *American Journal of Public Health, 105*, 463–469.

Sanger, C. (2022). Race, class, and reproductive rights: The impact of abortion restrictions. *Journal of Women, Politics & Policy, 43*, 487–505.

Shah, P. S., et al. (2011). Induced abortion and the risk of mental health outcomes: A systematic review of the literature. *The Journal of Psychiatry & Neuroscience, 36*, 137–145.

Siegel, R. B. (2022). The ethics of abortion and the changing legal landscape. *Harvard Law Review, 135*, 370–396.

Stone, G. R. (2022). The slippery slope argument and the reversal of Roe v. Wade. *Harvard Law Review, 135*, 1287–1304.

Thomson, J. J. (1971). A defense of abortion. *Philosophy & Public Affairs, 1*, 47–66.

World Health Organization. (2015). *Unsafe abortion: Global and regional estimates of the incidence of unsafe abortion and associated mortality in 2008* (6th ed.). World Health Organization.

Relevant Laws

Jennifer Toof

With contributions from Mandy McGuire Schwartz

As legislation surrounding abortion continues to evolve, it exerts profound implications not only on individuals seeking these services but also on the mental health professionals who support them. This chapter provides an overview of current laws related to abortion in different US states as well as laws that may specifically target or otherwise impact providers of mental health or social services. The chapter concludes with information on how professionals may navigate situations where there is a conflict between laws and ethical codes.

Laws: The Basics

It is vital that mental health professionals understand the basic concepts of the legal system and how certain laws affect their professional practice. The legal system is a structured framework of rules, institutions, and processes that govern a society's conduct. It is based on laws, which are a set of rules established by a governing authority to regulate the behavior of individuals and organizations within a society. Laws are different from professional ethical standards, which were discussed in depth in the previous chapter. Laws are intended to serve several critical functions, including maintaining order, protecting individual rights, resolving disputes, and promoting social justice. Laws are created through a legislative process, where elected representatives debate and pass bills that are then signed into law by an executive authority (e.g., the president or the governor). Once enacted, laws are enforced by various government agencies, such as the police and regulatory bodies, ensuring compliance through penalties or other legal consequences for violations. Laws are dynamic and can be amended or repealed to reflect societal changes, technological advancements, and evolving attitudes. In essence, laws function as a framework for societal conduct, balancing individual freedoms with the collective welfare, and are pivotal in fostering a stable and predictable environment.

Laws Related to Abortion

Currently, states vary widely in their approaches to abortion rights. In several states, abortions are now criminalized, meaning those who receive them could potentially be prosecuted. Even prior to the Dobbs decision, pregnant individuals could be prosecuted for fetal loss or harm in certain states under various laws, including chemical endangerment and fetal homicide laws. Examples include prosecution of those who, while pregnant, used substances, attempted suicide, or self-induced an abortion (Landess et al., 2023). Common restrictions related to reproductive rights include trigger bans (which were passed before the overturning of *Roe v. Wade* with the intention of banning abortion upon that happening), restrictions related to gestational age or viability, bans on particular abortion methods, and bans related to the reason for abortion (such as genetic anomaly, race, and sex) (Center for Reproductive Rights, 2024b). The Center for Reproductive Rights (2024b) has also identified abortion restrictions related to the Targeted Regulation of Abortion Providers (TRAP), concerning restrictions on which providers are allowed to provide abortion care, requirements regarding the notification or consent of the parents or guardians of young people seeking abortions, and requirements related to the conditions under which an individual seeking an abortion is deemed prepared to consent (e.g., after participating in counseling aimed at discouraging them from pursuing abortion, the use and discussion of ultrasounds or the monitoring of the fetal heartbeat, and waiting periods). Finally, other legal restrictions related to reproductive rights have targeted public funding (including coverage by the state Medicaid program and the provision of other funding to assist Medicaid recipients), requirements for the coverage of abortion by private insurance plans, the implementation of laws related to clinic safety and access, the expansion of the list of qualified medical providers who are allowed to provide abortion care, and interstate shield laws, which provide protection to abortion providers and helpers who work with out-of-state residents who travel to a state where abortion rights are protected (and in some cases also to their patients) (Center for Reproductive Rights, 2024b).

Legislation in Select States

To better understand reproductive rights legislation within the United States, it is helpful to look at the paths that have been taken within a few specific states. Below are summaries of some relevant legislation in the states of Texas, Wisconsin, New York, and Oregon, ranging from most to least restrictive in their current legislation related to abortion.

Texas

Dating back to 1854, according to the Texas State Law Library (2024c), the state of Texas made it a crime to attempt to "procure the miscarriage of any woman being with child." Between then and 1925, there were a number of updates to these statutes, codifying the Penal Code, renumbering the abortion statutes, and at times adding new language and small amendments. These early laws are now known, together, as the "1925 Laws." While these laws were deemed unconstitutional under Roe, they were never removed from the state statutes. Instead, going into effect in 1974, they were moved to the Revised Civil Statutes.

More recently, over the course of the twenty-two years prior to the Dobbs decision, a steady stream of new abortion restrictions have been put into place in the state of Texas. In his *Texas Tribune* article, Reynolds (2021) cataloged some of the major changes in Texas state legislation related to abortion during this period. In 2000, enforcement began for a 1999 parental notification law. This law required parental notification forty-eight hours before an abortion could be performed on a minor unless a judge granted an exception. With the 2003 passage of the "Women's Right to Know Act," a twenty-four-hour waiting period was required before all abortions, and abortions occurring after sixteen weeks of gestation were required to take place in a hospital or outpatient surgery center. In 2005, the parental notification law was tightened, and all abortions were banned after twenty-four weeks gestation. That year, the state also began providing funding to crisis pregnancy centers and other organizations providing pregnant patients with counseling advising them against abortion. In 2011, further legislation required a sonogram within twenty-four hours before an abortion, with the further requirement that a doctor review the sonogram with the pregnant patient, discuss fetal development, and make the fetal heartbeat (if present) audible to the patient. In 2011, there were also tax dollar restrictions put into place, preventing Texas agencies from using tax dollars for any expenses related to abortions and forbidding them from contracting with facilities providing abortions. In 2013, further restrictions were imposed, banning abortions after twenty weeks postfertilization with few exceptions, requiring all abortion facilities (even those providing abortion only via the administration of pills) to meet the standard of ambulatory surgical centers, putting into place a required state protocol for medication abortion, and requiring physicians performing abortions to have admitting privileges at a hospital within 30 miles of the facility.

In 2017, the most frequently used procedure for second-trimester abortions was banned in Texas. However, this law was prevented from going into effect following a legal challenge by advocates for abortion rights based on the legislation presenting "an undue burden to the right to abortion" (Reynolds, 2021). Also in 2017, insurance companies were restricted from including abortion care under comprehensive health insurance plans. In 2019, criminal penalties were instituted for any abortion provider who did not provide medical care to a fetus born after an abortion. Reynolds (2021) noted that this is an unlikely scenario, as fetal viability begins at twenty-four weeks, and abortions after twenty weeks had already been banned in the state of Texas. Starting in 2019, government entities were prevented from providing assistance to clinics associated with abortion providers. This resulted in the elimination of government assistance to low-cost health clinics that were affiliated with abortion providers, even if there were no abortion services provided in those locations. Finally, the Texas "heartbeat" law of 2021, based on Senate Bill 8, banned all abortions starting at the time when fetal cardiac activity can first be detected by ultrasound, usually around six weeks gestation. This legislation also allowed private individuals to sue abortion providers that violate this ban (Reynolds, 2021). That same year, House Bill 1280, which included a "trigger" provision banning abortion following the overturning or limitation of the Roe ruling, was also passed into law (Texas State Law Library, 2024c).

Based on the many restrictions on abortion that went into effect in the state of Texas in the years prior to Dobbs, access to abortion was already quite limited for many Texans during that period. According to the Center for Reproductive Rights (2024a), as of 2017, ten of the twenty-seven US "cities classified as 'abortion deserts'—where residents need to travel 100 miles or more to reach a provider"—were in Texas. Further, in 2017, there was not a single provider of abortion services in 96 percent of Texas counties (Center for Reproductive Rights, 2024a).

According to the Texas State Law Library (2024a), in August of 2022, shortly after the Dobbs ruling, Texas Health and Safety Code, Chapter 170A, went into effect, based on House Bill 1280, prohibiting almost all abortions in the state. Under this statute, there are no exceptions for cases of rape or incest. There is, however, an exception in the event of risks to the life or health of the pregnant individual. There are also civil penalties for those who perform an abortion.

Around that same time, the state's earlier "1925 Laws" were also revived. After the Dobbs decision, the Attorney General of Texas, Ken Paxton, suggested that these laws could still be enforced (Texas State Law Library, 2024c). Paxton was then sued by a group of clinics who sought a restraining order to prevent this. A judge granted a temporary restraining order, resulting in Paxton seeking an emergency stay of the order from the Texas Supreme Court. A stay order was issued on July 1, 2022, "temporarily permitting the enforcement of the laws while the court considers the case" (Texas State Law Library, 2024c). For as long as this is the case, anyone providing an abortion in the state of Texas may thus be found criminally liable. However, doctors, pharmacists, and pharmacies have been provided with some protection by House Bill 3058, which took effect in September 2023. This legislation provides legal protection to physicians who terminate a pregnancy to prevent certain life-threatening complications (Texas State Law Library, 2024b).

Wisconsin

Like Texas, the state of Wisconsin first passed legislation prohibiting abortion in the nineteenth century. In Wisconsin, this law was passed in 1849, specifically prohibiting abortion after "quickening," the point at which the pregnant individual can feel the fetus moving in utero (typically about halfway through the pregnancy). Subsequent changes to state law in 1858 have been interpreted as extending the ban to all stages of pregnancy. Also in 1858, a second legal offense was created, establishing penalties for anyone who helped someone obtain an abortion (Claflin, 2024). The question of the relevance of quickening was settled in 1923 when the Wisconsin Supreme Court ruled that charges of manslaughter could only be applied if the fetus had reached the stage of quickening. The ruling included the statement that a "'two months' embryo is not a human being in the eye of the law" (Claflin, 2024). The language in this legislation was revised in the 1950s, making it a felony to either kill an unborn child or kill "the mother with the intent of destroying her unborn child" (Associated Press, 2024). Revisions made to state law at that time also made it permissible for a doctor working in consultation with two other doctors to perform an abortion in an attempt to save the mother's life (Associated Press, 2024).

As in Texas, after the *Roe v. Wade* ruling made abortion legal nationwide, legislators in Wisconsin never repealed the state's earlier legislation banning abortion. Also like Texas, after the Dobbs case was decided, there was a discussion in Wisconsin about whether the previous restrictions could be enforced again. Unlike in Texas, however, Wisconsin state legislation passed in the years after Roe was codified included both the implementation of further restrictions and at least the potential for some protections. Some legislation in 1985 prohibited abortions occurring after the point of fetal viability but seemingly allowed for abortions occurring prior to that point (Associated

Press, 2024). In 2015, a bill was signed into law that banned abortions after twenty weeks gestation, with no exceptions for rape or incest but an exception for medical necessity. This legislation also stated that physicians in violation of this ban could be convicted of a felony (Claflin, 2024). Additional restrictions that have been incorporated into the state statutes include a requirement for in-person counseling at least twenty-four hours before an abortion, a requirement for an ultrasound even if not medically necessary, a requirement that medication abortion occur in person, a requirement of parental consent for minors, the restriction of state Medicaid coverage for abortion to only very limited circumstances, the requirement that abortions be performed only by physicians, and the implementation of additional regulations for abortion clinics. Wisconsin state law does, however, also provide some protection from physical harm and harassment for those who enter an abortion clinic (Guttmacher Institute, 2024c).

Following the Dobbs decision in 2022, there was initially uncertainty as to whether the old legislation banning abortion in Wisconsin would stand. During a fifteen-month period, all abortion services in the state were halted (Claflin, 2024). Additionally in 2022, Wisconsin Attorney General Josh Kaul, a Democrat, filed a lawsuit arguing that the 1985 law allowing abortions before the point of fetal viability superseded the ban. The Republican District Attorney of Sheboygan County, Joel Urmanski, meanwhile, argued that the 1849 ban should still be enforceable (Associated Press, 2024).

In 2023, Dane County Circuit Judge Diane Schlipper ruled that the old ban applied to feticide without the consent of the pregnant individual, but not to consensual abortions. Based on this ruling, Planned Parenthood began to offer abortions in the state of Wisconsin again. These deliberations have continued to be hotly contested since that time. In February 2024, Urmanski requested that the state Supreme Court overturn Schlipper's 2023 ruling, without waiting for the ruling of the lower appellate courts. In July 2024, the Supreme Court agreed to take the case. Meanwhile, in February 2024, a separate lawsuit, filed by Planned Parenthood of Wisconsin, asked the state Supreme Court "to rule directly on whether a constitutional right to abortion exists in the state" (Associated Press, 2024). The state Supreme Court agreed in July 2024 to take this case, as well.

As of November 2024, abortion services were available at health centers in the cities of Madison, Milwaukee, and Sheboygan. The state legislature, which has a Republican majority, has tried to further limit abortion access but has not succeeded in passing legislation, which would face veto by Governor Tony Evers. Evers, a Democrat, has expressed commitment to maintaining access to abortion. The state Supreme Court, which has had a liberal majority since 2023, is also currently viewed as favoring the protection of reproductive rights (Claflin, 2024).

New York

Like many other states, the state of New York passed several laws restricting reproductive rights in the nineteenth century. According to Makert (1990), in 1828, the state criminalized the abortion of a "quick" fetus, considering this to be second-degree manslaughter. This legislation also made it a misdemeanor to try to obtain a miscarriage at any point in a pregnancy except when necessary to save the life of the pregnant individual. A new law passed in 1845 indicated that individuals seeking abortion would also be deemed guilty of manslaughter. In 1869, the state made abortion at any stage of development a misdemeanor. The following year, it made it a felony to cause the death of a fetus or a woman via abortion. Additionally, this legislation made it a felony to obtain an abortion.

However, New York legalized abortion without residency requirements in 1970, three years before the Roe decision (Center for Reproductive Rights, 2024c). Further, reproductive rights protections in the state of New York have since been bolstered through the enactment of a series of subsequent state laws. In 2019, the state passed comprehensive abortion rights legislation, enacting protection for abortion and other reproductive health care decisions as fundamental rights under state law. In 2022, additional protections for abortion providers and helpers were added to the statutes. Moreover, in 2024, voters approved the Equal Rights Amendment, which amended the state constitution to prohibit discrimination based on factors including pregnancy outcome.

According to the Guttmacher Institute (2024a), abortion policies in the state of New York are currently considered "very protective." While abortion is banned at twenty-four weeks, there are also many protections and supports for abortion providers and those they serve. Abortion services are covered by state Medicaid funds, and private health care plans are also required to provide coverage for abortion care. There are also state funds that may be used to help defray the cost of abortion. Abortions may be performed by qualified health care professionals including but not limited to physicians. There are state protections against harassment and physical harm for those entering an abortion clinic. Finally, there is a shield law that protects those who provide abortions and may also cover patients as well as organizations providing support services.

Oregon

Though Oregon, too, had some early legislation banning abortion, this ban was repealed in 1983, at which time the right to abortion was written into the state constitution (Center for Reproductive Rights, 2024d; Oregon Health & Science University, 2024). Further protections and resources related to abortion rights have also been implemented in the state. The Reproductive Health Equity Act was passed in 2017, protecting the access of all Oregon residents, regardless of income or citizenship status, to family planning services, abortion, and postpartum care. Legislators also set aside $15 million to provide abortion providers with funding to hire more staff, buy equipment, and expand services (Oregon Health & Science University, 2024). In 2022, the state legislature set aside an additional $15 million, in this case appropriating it to the Reproductive Health Equity Fund, to provide support including travel expenses for those seeking abortions in Oregon (Center for Reproductive Rights, 2024d).

In 2023, the state deemed abortion a fundamental right. At the same time, the state enacted an interstate shield law and also specified that young people under the age of fifteen could consent to abortion care (Center for Reproductive Rights, 2024d). In Oregon in 2024, abortion care was available regardless of gestational duration. The cost of abortion services is covered by both Medicaid funds and private health insurance plans, and there is also a state fund to help individuals pay for abortion care. Abortion care can be provided by qualified health care professionals, including but not limited to physicians. Protections are also provided to those entering an abortion clinic as well as to providers (Guttmacher Institute, 2024b).

Laws Impacting Providers

As of the writing of this book, the main targets of laws related to reproductive rights appear to be individuals seeking to obtain an abortion and the medical providers who provide such procedures (American Psychological Association [APA], 2022). Following the reversal of *Roe v. Wade*, medical providers such as obstetricians and gynecologists in some parts of the country could face direct liability for their role in reproductive care if it may be considered aiding and abetting a criminal to help an individual receive an abortion. Could other providers, such as psychiatrists, psychologists, and counselors, face possible criminal prosecution for providing referrals to clients interested in obtaining an abortion, knowing that a client is going to have an abortion and not informing authorities, or even for discussing abortion with their clients?

Just as several states were profiled in this chapter with regard to if/how their abortion laws impact those who receive or perform abortions, several states are also described below with regard to if/how their abortion laws may impact mental health professionals. As previously discussed, laws related to reproductive rights vary considerably between states and are in a constant state of flux. This text should in no way be considered legal advice. Mental health professionals should maintain ongoing awareness of the various laws that may impact their work with clients and consult with legal professionals, their licensing board(s), and their liability carrier as needed. Laws should be considered in both the state(s) in which the provider practices as well as the state in which the client lives if these are not the same.

Ohio

As described in Chapter 2 discussing responses to the overturning of *Roe v. Wade*, Lebanon, Ohio, had a ban in place that could criminalize advocates, social workers, or other mental health professionals for providing assistance to residents accessing abortion care (National Association of Social Workers [NASW], 2023). The ordinance made it illegal to help persons in the city obtain abortions outside Lebanon, where abortion is illegal. It criminalized a wide range of potential activities that could be considered aiding and abetting, such as providing transportation, instructions, money, and even services that could be considered emotional support to people seeking abortions. In response, the NASW and Abortion Fund of Ohio brought a lawsuit against the city, claiming the ordinance violated constitutionally protected rights. They succeeded in having the ordinance amended. As a result of the lawsuit, individuals in Lebanon, Ohio, would no longer face prosecution for helping people obtain lawful abortions outside of the city (NASW, 2023). Danielle Smith, executive director of NASW Ohio, said:

> We are proud to have defeated Lebanon's attempt to criminalize social workers for simply doing their jobs. Prior to our successful litigation, social workers across Ohio were at risk of being sent to jail not only for helping people access essential health care but even just for providing therapeutic space for clients to talk about abortion. This is a critical victory in ensuring our clients receive quality ethical care. (NASW, 2023)

Texas

In Texas, under Senate Bill 8, which took effect in 2021, individuals may sue anyone who helped someone to have an abortion. When a plaintiff wins a civil suit of this kind, the courts are to award them at least $10,000 in damages from the defendants (Bowman, 2022). The states of Idaho and Oklahoma included similar provisions in their abortion bans, modeled after Texas Senate Bill 8. According to law professor Mary Ziegler, provisions like these, which focus on a system of enforcement through civil lawsuits, may be more effective than criminal laws (Bowman, 2022). Criminal laws, like those finding abortion providers or patients legally liable, may be more subject to court challenges, as well as inconsistent enforcement by prosecutors.

There have been legal challenges to Texas Senate Bill 8, including a state suit brought by a social worker and another brought by a donor to women's health clinics, as well as a federal suit brought by twenty abortion providers (Glynn, 2021). To date, however, the law has remained in place. This law can have a direct impact on the work of many mental health and social services professionals. As the Texas abortion ban has no exceptions for cases of rape or incest, those who work with survivors of sexual abuse and assault may be affected to a particularly large extent. According to social worker Monica Faulkner, who filed one of the suits against the state of Texas, many colleagues who work with survivors of sexual violence have voiced concerns about how much they can say about the option of abortion without risking being sued (Glynn, 2021). She noted, "It's just a really heavy burden for people who are on the frontlines right now" (Lopez, 2021).

Kentucky

In some cases, public opposition has prevented certain provisions from being enacted. For example, in Kentucky in 2023, the American Counseling Association (ACA) and the Kentucky Counseling Association joined with other state associations representing mental health workers, psychologists, and social workers to oppose a bill that would have criminalized counseling that included discussion related to abortion. Ultimately, the bill was not passed (Marsalek, 2023).

Indiana

There have been concerns that in some states mental health professionals may be required to report instances of patients experiencing negative psychological effects after having abortions (Landess et al., 2023). The state of Indiana has such legislation in place, requiring clinicians to report adverse abortion outcomes including suicidality and depression. However, the constitutionality of this law has been called into question, partly related to the difficulty of determining causality between an abortion and a particular clinical outcome.

Tennessee

Tennessee's trigger ban made abortions in the state illegal, with few exceptions, after Roe was overturned, meaning that people seeking abortions would need to travel out of state. In April 2024, the Tennessee State Senate passed a bill that created the new crime of "abortion trafficking," meaning that any adult who helped a minor obtain an abortion without parental consent could face mandatory jail time as well as civil lawsuits for the fetus's wrongful death (Wadhwani, 2024b). Specifically, the bill criminalized recruiting, harboring, or transporting a pregnant unemancipated minor to obtain an abortion, including via an abortion-inducing drug, without written notarized consent from the parent or guardian. The bill also criminalized adults "concealing" or "procuring" minors' abortions, language that Democratic Tennessee State Senator Jeff Yarbro called "so remarkably unclear it could apply to almost anyone to whom a pregnant minor turns to discuss [their] options" (Wadhwani, 2024b, para. 9). He further stated:

> Under the legislation as drafted, I'm not sure you can have an honest conversation with your grandparents, with your older sibling who's an adult, with your priest, with your pastor, with an attorney, with a mental health provider. The communications themselves are potentially a criminal act here. (Wadhwani, 2024b, para. 10)

Opponents of the bill noted that it would be particularly harmful to minors who became pregnant as a result of rape/incest, as they may not feel safe or comfortable speaking to their parents (Wadhwani, 2024b). A lawsuit challenging the bill was filed by Tennessee State Representative Aftyn Behn, a Nashville Democrat and social worker who has publicly advocated for abortion rights (Wadhwani, 2024b). In September 2024, a federal judge temporarily blocked enforcement of the law, concluding that it was likely an unconstitutional ban on free speech and agreeing that the language in the bill was "so ill-defined it could encompass a wide range of conversations about abortion, including simply telling a pregnant teen about all [their] options" (Wadhwani, 2024a, para. 3).

When discussing relevant legislation in Tennessee that may impact mental health providers, it is important to note that Tennessee is one of several US states that has "conscience clauses" allowing therapists to refuse services to a client if such services conflict with the therapist's "sincerely held principles," including religious beliefs (Grzanka & Frantell, 2017). As previously described in this text, religious beliefs and thoughts on abortion are closely related. Thus, under this law, a therapist who is against abortion for religious reasons could refuse services to a client who has had or is considering an abortion. Per Grzanka and Frantell (2017), conscience clauses directly enable discrimination against particular groups of clients and hinder access to care. Additionally, a therapist may not know that a client has had or is considering an abortion and therefore not realize the conflict between their own beliefs and the client's concerns until several or even many sessions into the relationship. Thus, it can become even more ethically troublesome to terminate an existing client–therapist relationship (Grzanka & Frantell, 2017). Although Tennessee's conscience clause requires that a referral to an alternative provider be made, there is no guarantee that a referral can be made to a reasonable, affordable, or geographically close provider. Due to concerns about the discriminatory nature of conscience clauses, national organizations such as the APA and the ACA have issued statements rebuking the direct conflict with their ethics codes, specifically the ethical obligation of nondiscrimination and avoiding harming a client (Grzanka & Frantell, 2017).

American Psychological Association FAQs

The APA (2022, para. 4) wrote that "while the situation [regarding reproductive rights] is dynamic, good psychological practice remains unchanged." This means that, despite the changing laws regarding access to reproductive health care, mental health professionals' responsibilities to prioritize their patients' or clients' welfare should not change. The organization compiled a comprehensive list of frequently asked questions for providers with questions about changing abortion laws, some of which are summarized below.

1. Am I practicing in a state where abortion is, or soon will be, illegal under all or certain circumstances?

As previously stated, laws can change often, so staying up-to-date on the laws in the state(s) where you practice is vital. For a list of existing abortion bans and restrictions within each US state, the Center for Reproductive Rights has a map that is updated in real time on their website. Additionally, the Guttmacher Institute's website provides information about abortion-related laws around the country (APA, 2022).

2. What are the risks of talking with patients/clients about, or providing them with, resources for how to obtain an abortion if my state bans or restricts them?

While laws related to aiding and abetting individuals in obtaining abortions generally do not target mental health professionals, providers should take care to ensure they are not involved in activities that could be considered directly connected to helping an individual obtain an abortion in states where abortions are banned or heavily restricted. Indeed, there could be legal risks to giving out specific information about how to obtain an abortion in such states. For instance, referring someone to a specific abortion clinic, helping them make an appointment, providing them with transportation or financial assistance for an abortion, or other actions could be considered aiding and abetting. Texas and other states that have criminalized abortion have already passed laws specifically expanding abortion liability for those who help facilitate an abortion. For example, Texas's "bounty hunter" law also went into effect in September 2021, offering strong incentives ($10,000) for people to bring lawsuits against anyone aiding or abetting an illegal abortion. The APA (2022), however, noted that they were unaware of any such cases being brought against psychologists and added that aiding and abetting laws are being challenged in court.

Providers should also remember that they must ethically practice within their scope of practice. Stepping outside of one's regular professional role by providing specific forms of assistance in helping patients/clients receive an abortion could create malpractice concerns. Instead, providers may consider reducing risk by providing more general information or resources to patients/clients (APA, 2022).

3. Can I talk to my patients/clients about the mental health implications of getting or not getting an abortion?

Providers may be concerned about discussing any issues related to abortion with patients/clients living in states with bans or restrictions. At the time of writing, the APA (2022) had not become aware of any mental health professionals facing legal liability for providing general mental health services to people considering abortions. Mental health professionals are trusted sources of reliable information regarding mental health issues, so it behooves professionals to be sufficiently informed of the mental health effects an individual may experience when considering getting or not getting an abortion. Providers should take steps to ensure they deliver accurate information about mental health implications based on research and be mindful that personal biases do not affect the information they give out. Per the APA (2022), professionals should also make sure they are respecting their patients' or clients' autonomy and help them come to a decision that is most appropriate for them as opposed to making the decision for their patients or clients.

4. If my patient/client is considering or had an abortion that is illegal in their state, am I required to report it?

Certain states require abortion-related reporting, but these laws currently apply only to providers or facilities performing abortions. At the time of writing, no US state requires mental health professionals to report someone who intends to have an abortion or who has had an abortion. However, in states with fetal personhood laws, where the definition of "child" or "person" now extends to fetuses, mental health professionals may have concerns about their mandatory reporting requirements surrounding child abuse or duty-to-warn responsibilities (APA, 2022; Landess et al., 2023). For example, if a mental health professional learns that someone intends to obtain an illegal abortion or to otherwise engage in acts likely to result in fetal harm, new laws could require them to warn authorities in order to protect the fetus (Landess et al., 2023). Currently, the US Department of Health and Human Services Office of Civil Rights recently confirmed that the HIPAA Privacy Rule would not permit disclosure of patient information related to abortion under mandatory abuse or duty-to-warn reporting (APA, 2022).

As always, providers should always discuss confidentiality, limits of confidentiality, and potential duty-to-report obligations in their state with their patients or clients. That way, the patient/client can decide whether they may want to avoid talking about certain topics, such as abortion, that may require a mental health professional to break confidentiality (APA, 2022). Since mandated reporting requirements may present complex ethical challenges, consultation with one's state licensing board or malpractice carrier may be indicated (Landess et al., 2023).

5. What happens if a court or law enforcement agent in a state with an abortion ban seeks the mental health records of a patient/client who received an abortion?

The APA (2022) did not find records of prosecutors, law enforcement, or state agencies seeking mental health records for abortion prosecutions. Generally, patient/client records or information may be handed over in response to a subpoena only with consent from the patient/client due to psychotherapist–patient or counselor–client privilege. Asserting this privilege could provide grounds for not divulging confidential information. The APA (2022) recommends that, if providers find themselves in a situation where a legal body seeks to compel disclosure of confidential information related to abortion, they should contact their malpractice carrier and an attorney familiar with this situation who is authorized to practice in their state. Again, mental health professionals should remind patients/clients about the limits of confidentiality and privilege and the possibly evolving laws on what may be shared with others.

6. Should I change my documentation/recordkeeping practices to protect my patients/clients when they talk about abortion?

Both the APA (2022) and Landess et al. (2023) noted that providers should always use good clinical judgment when documenting sensitive matters in patient/client records. Providers should consider the potential consequences of including certain information in the documentation and consider utilizing language such as "health care decisions" or "family issues" as opposed to "abortion" (APA, 2022).

7. What if I'm providing services via telehealth from a state where abortion is legal to someone in a state where abortion is illegal?

Mental health professionals must always be aware of the laws not only in the states where they are located but also in the states where they see clients, and this is especially true for issues surrounding abortion-related laws due to the potential for significant differences from one state to another. If the patient/client lives in a state where abortion is illegal or heavily restricted, the provider should consider the suggestions described in responses to other questions. The APA (2022) wrote that it could be difficult for out-of-state prosecutors to subpoena a mental health professional's records if the provider is in another state that does not have abortion restrictions. Some of these states have also passed laws restricting how health care records are accessed across state lines (APA, 2022). Again, however, laws are likely to continue to change, so staying informed and seeking professional consultation/legal advice may be needed in situations that are unclear to the provider.

8. How can I voice my personal thoughts about the overturning of *Roe v. Wade* without incurring legal risk?

As described in the chapter on the ethical responsibilities of mental health professionals, it is important to adhere to one's code of ethics when providing professional services regardless of one's stance on abortion. The APA (2022) recommended that providers make their voices heard on their own time by engaging in advocacy efforts, such as supporting candidates, contacting elected officials, getting involved with federal, state, or local legislative efforts, and donating to organizations that support one's position.

Conflicts between Ethical Codes and Laws

When it comes to reproductive rights, the divisive and developing nature of the subject means that providers may encounter conflicts between their professional ethical codes and changing legislation. As described in the chapter on ethics, per the ACA's (ACA, 2014) *Code of Ethics*, if there is a conflict between ethical codes and law, counselors must make known their commitment to the ethics code and take steps to resolve the conflict. Standard I.1.c of the code states that "counselors, acting in the best interests of the client, may adhere to the requirements of the law, regulations, and/or other governing legal authority" (ACA, 2014). Several ethical decision-making models were outlined in the previous chapter. Below, another model that incorporates legal decision-making is discussed. Additionally, key conflicts between ethical codes and laws are examined, with potential solutions considered.

Using a Legal and Ethical Decision-Making Model

At times, ethics and laws can conflict on the same topic. In these instances, it is important to consider both ethics and laws when counselors make decisions regarding the care of their clients. Wheeler and Bertram (2019, p. 9) developed a legal and ethical decision-making model to help counselors navigate situations that may involve both ethical and legal considerations or where there is a conflict between laws and ethical standards. The approach is intended to be deliberate, explicit, and logical and to "yield defensible results when counselors are faced with explaining their decision-making process." When faced with situations involving abortion-related laws, mental health professionals may consider utilizing this model, the steps to which are summarized below:

1. Define the problem, dilemma, and sub-issues. This step entails examining the core concerns—legal, ethical, clinical, or a combination. For example, the dilemma may be between what is legal, what is ethical, and what is in the client's best interests (Wheeler & Bertram, 2019).

2. Identify the client's worldview. In this step, the counselor seeks to understand contextual and environmental factors that contribute to the client's worldview and if/how they influence the client (Wheeler & Bertram, 2019). These factors may include intersecting variables such as race, religion, and socioeconomic status. With regard to reproductive rights, these factors may have a strong influence on both the client's personal beliefs about abortion as well as on their ability to access abortion. Wheeler and Bertram (2019) noted that recognizing the client's worldview is a way for the counselor to demonstrate respect for them as the counselor works through the decision-making process.

3. Review/understand the laws, ethical codes, and institutional policies (if applicable) that pertain to the dilemma (Wheeler & Bertram, 2019). As previously discussed, when it comes to abortion, legislation varies from state to state and may be in a constant state of flux. Thus, counselors should not rely on memory to inform them of laws (or ethical codes/institutional policies) but should know how or where they can access up-to-date information and, if needed, consult with appropriate parties to ensure a thorough understanding of the laws/codes/policies (Wheeler & Bertram, 2019).

4. Be alert to personal influences. In this step, the counselor should seek to determine what personal values, bias/prejudice, or countertransference may be affecting perception (Wheeler & Bertram, 2019). As abortion is a topic that most people feel strongly about one way or the other, the counselor must ensure that their personal feelings about abortion do not influence the way they handle the situation. Per Wheeler and Bertram (2019), the point here is not that counselors should not have values, biases, prejudices, or moments of countertransference, but that, when engaged in a legal or ethical decision-making process, they must examine the potential impacts of them.

5. Obtain an outside perspective. In this step, the counselor should engage in colleague consultation and/or supervision as well as obtain legal advice from a professional (Wheeler & Bertram, 2019).

6. Enumerate options and consequences. This step involves identifying the various courses of action and the intended and unintended consequences of each (Wheeler & Bertram, 2019).

7. Decide and take action. This penultimate step is where the counselor implements the decision they selected while being prepared to reconsider options (Wheeler & Bertram, 2019).

8. Finally, the counselor should document their decision-making and follow-up actions so that there is written evidence of the steps they took and the ensuing results (Wheeler & Bertram, 2019). Careful documentation helps the counselor demonstrate that they took a deliberate and logical approach to the decision-making process and can help them justify the decision to other bodies, if necessary.

Key Conflicts and Potential Solutions

In discussing the potential conflicts between ethical codes and laws regarding abortion, it is important to recognize that these two domains can often have divergent principles and guidelines. Some key conflicts may include, but are not limited to, the following: autonomy versus legal restrictions; beneficence and nonmaleficence versus legal limitations; confidentiality versus mandatory reporting laws; and justice versus socioeconomic barriers. Below, these conflicts are explored, with potential solutions briefly addressed. Readers are encouraged to consider other possible ways of addressing these and other conflicts.

Autonomy and legal restrictions may conflict with each other, as ethical codes often emphasize the importance of respecting individual autonomy, including a person's right to make decisions about their own body, while abortion bans may be seen as limiting this autonomy. However, legal systems may impose restrictions on abortion, limiting this autonomy. As a solution, mental health professionals may focus on their role in promoting autonomy within clients and if/how they can advocate for or contribute to conversations regarding the autonomy of the populations they serve.

Beneficence (acting in the best interests of clients) and nonmaleficence (doing no harm) could conflict with legal limitations on abortion. For example, abortion-related laws may force providers to withhold valuable services or resources to the clients they serve. Mental health professionals should continue to act in the best interests of their clients in the ways that they know they can. Additionally, they may advocate for laws or legal exceptions that allow mental health care providers to act according to their ethical obligations in circumstances where the client's mental or physical health is at risk.

As previously discussed, mandatory reporting laws that may require providers to report abortions could cause tremendous concern for providers whose ethical codes prioritize confidentiality. Providers should always discuss potential limits of confidentiality with clients, thereby giving clients the power to decide what or how much to share in sessions. On the advocacy front, mental health providers may work toward legal reforms that protect confidentiality while balancing any need for mandatory reporting.

An earlier chapter in this book detailed how abortion regulations can negatively impact mental health and how they disproportionately affect marginalized groups. Many professional ethical codes stress justice and equity in health care access; thus, a conflict between the concept of justice and laws that create socioeconomic barriers to abortion may exist. As a possible solution, mental health professionals may work to ensure that their own services are accessible to individuals from diverse backgrounds and socioeconomic statuses and that these clients receive the same level of care and consideration regardless of their identities. Moreover, providers can speak out against discriminatory practices or laws and advocate for policies that ensure equitable access to both mental and physical health care, including reproductive health care.

In summary, mental health professionals can take action both in and outside of the therapy room to ensure the well-being of those they serve. These actions may include, but are not limited to, the following: creating a safe space in therapy sessions where clients feel safe to express feelings/concerns about abortion; engaging in continued education and training about the legal, medical, and psychological aspects of abortion and related issues; and advocating for clients' rights/supporting legislation that is in their client's best interests. Indeed, advocacy is often mentioned as an expectation of ethical advocacy for professionals. For example, the ACA (ACA, 2014) *Code of Ethics* states that "counselors are expected to advocate to promote changes at the individual, group, institutional, and societal levels that improve the quality of life for individuals and groups and remove potential barriers to the provision or access of appropriate services being offered." The various actions mental health professionals can take, which are described further in the final chapter of this text, can help them play a vital role in supporting their clients' reproductive decisions, promoting mental well-being, and contributing to broader systemic changes related to abortion access and rights.

Conclusion

Mental health professionals may be affected by legislation related to reproductive rights not only directly, in their own personal lives, but also professionally, as this legislation affects their clients and their communities. Beyond these impacts, there have also been concerns that some laws related to abortion may have legal implications for the work of mental health professionals. Thus, it is incumbent upon these professionals to stay abreast of all laws that could impact the work they do and seek legal guidance when necessary. Additionally, mental health professionals should strive to utilize a sound ethical and legal decision-making model when needed to reduce conflicts and improve outcomes for all parties involved. Finally, advocating for legislation that is in the best interest of the clients they serve is a valuable way for mental health professionals to make their voices heard and influence positive change that can lead to improved mental health outcomes for individuals and communities.

Discussion Questions

1) What are the laws regarding abortion and reproductive rights in your state?

2) How do you think you can stay informed on changing legislation related to reproductive rights?
3) What other legal questions/concerns might you have regarding how abortion-related laws could impact your clients?
4) What other legal questions/concerns might you have regarding how abortion-related laws could impact your professional practice?

References

American Counseling Association. (2014). *2014 ACA code of ethics.* https://www.counseling.org/knowledge-center/ethics

American Psychological Association. (2022, September 1). *Frequently asked questions about abortion laws and psychology practice.* https://www.apaservices.org/practice/business/hipaa/abortion-laws

Associated Press. (2024, November 11). Wisconsin high court to hear arguments on whether an 1849 abortion ban remains valid. *NPR.* https://www.npr.org/2024/11/11/g-s1-33658/wisconsin-high-court-abortion-ban

Bowman, E. (2022, July 11). As states ban abortion, the Texas bounty law offers a way to survive legal challenges. *NPR.* https://www.npr.org/2022/07/11/1107741175/texas-abortion-bounty-law

Center for Reproductive Rights. (2024a). *Abortion in texas.* https://reproductiverights.org/case/texas-abortion-ban-us-supreme-court/abortion-in-texas

Center for Reproductive Rights. (2024b). *After Roe fell: Abortion laws by state.* https://reproductiverights.org/maps/abortion-laws-by-state/

Center for Reproductive Rights. (2024c). *After Roe fell: Abortion laws by state: New York.* https://reproductiverights.org/maps/state/new-york/

Center for Reproductive Rights. (2024d). *After Roe fell: Abortion laws by state: Oregon.* https://reproductiverights.org/maps/state/oregon/

Claflin, H. (2024, July 1). Wisconsin's convoluted history of abortion laws. *Wisconsin Watch.* https://wisconsinwatch.org/2024/07/wisconsin-supreme-court-abortion-constitution-law-pregnancy-roe-wade/

Glynn, M. (2021, August 31). *Social workers, lawyers of sexual assault victims file lawsuits against Texas' fetal heartbeat bill. KTAL NBC 6.* https://www.ktalnews.com/news/texas/texas-politics/social-workers-lawyers-of-sexual-assault-victims-file-lawsuits-against-texas-fetal-heartbeat-bill/

Grzanka, P. R., & Frantell, K. A. (2017). Counseling psychology and reproductive justice: A call to action. *The Counseling Psychologist, 45*(3), 326–352. https://doi.org/10.1177/0011000017699871

Guttmacher Institute. (2024a). *Interactive map: US abortion policies and access after Roe: New York.* https://states.guttmacher.org/policies/new-york/abortion-policies

Guttmacher Institute. (2024b). *Interactive map: US abortion policies and access after Roe: Oregon.* https://states.guttmacher.org/policies/oregon/abortion-policies

Guttmacher Institute. (2024c). *Interactive map: US abortion policies and access after Roe: Wisconsin.* https://states.guttmacher.org/policies/wisconsin/abortion-policies

Landess, J., Hatters-Friedman, S., Kaempf, A., & Ross, N. (2023). Abortion and the psychiatrist: Practicing in post-Dobbs America. *The Psychiatric Times, 40*(1). https://www.psychiatrictimes.com/view/abortion-and-the-psychiatrist-practicing-in-post-dobbs-america

Lopez, A. (2021, October 18). Social workers warn Texas' abortion ban is causing psychological harm to sexual assault survivors. *Texas Public Radio.* https://www.tpr.org/government-politics/2021-10-18/social-workers-warn-texas-abortion-ban-is-causing-psychological-harm-to-sexual-assault-survivors

Makert, K. Z. (1990, January 16). *To bear or not to bear: Abortion in Victorian America.* http://hdl.handle.net/10822/1051350

Marsalek, D. N. (2023, June). Advocacy update: Collaborating for change. *Counseling Today.* https://www.counseling.org/publications/counseling-today-magazine/article-archive/article/legacy/advocacy-update-collaborating-for-change

National Association of Social Workers. (2023, January 12). *Abortion & reproductive health.* https://www.naswoh.org/page/abortion

Oregon Health & Science University. (2024). *Breaking barriers: Access to abortion care in Oregon.* https://www.ohsu.edu/womens-health/breaking-barriers-access-abortion-care-oregon#

Reynolds, K. (2021, November 1). How today's near-total abortion ban in Texas was 20 years in the making. *The Texas Tribune.* https://www.texastribune.org/2021/11/01/Texas-abortion-restrictions-timeline/

Texas State Law Library. (2024a, November 21). *Abortion laws.* https://guides.sll.texas.gov/abortion-laws

Texas State Law Library. (2024b, November 21). *Civil penalties.* https://guides.sll.texas.gov/abortion-laws/civil-penalties

Texas State Law Library. (2024c, November 21). *History of abortion laws.* https://guides.sll.texas.gov/abortion-laws/history-of-abortion-laws

Wadhwani, A. (2024a, September 24). Judge blocks Tennessee law that bans helping a minor get an abortion without parental consent. *Tennessee Lookout.* https://tennesseelookout.com/2024/09/24/judge-blocks-tennessee-law-that-bans-helping-a-minor-get-an-abortion-without-parental-consent/

Wadhwani, A. (2024b, April 11). Tennessee Senate passes bill making it a crime to aid a minor seeking an abortion. *Tennessee Lookout.* https://tennesseelookout.com/2024/04/11/senate-passes-bill-making-it-a-crime-to-aid-a-minor-seeking-an-abortion/

Wheeler, A. M., & Bertram, B. (2019). *The counselor and the law: A guide to legal and ethical practice* (8th ed.). American Counseling Association.

Responsibilities and Implications for Mental Health Professionals

Jennifer Toof and Ami Crowley

With contributions from Mehj Aubol Khan and Erin-Lee Kelly

Now that the reader has gained a familiarity with the mental health impacts of the overturning of *Roe v. Wade*, as well as with relevant professional ethics codes and laws, this chapter will further examine the legal, ethical, and social justice responsibilities of and implications for mental health professionals. This chapter will describe implications for clinical practice, education/supervision, research, and advocacy.

Staying Informed

One of the first and most important responsibilities of mental health professionals is to stay informed regarding how the overturning of *Roe v. Wade* and subsequent legislation may impact clients and the work they do. Clients often seek information from mental health professionals, so it is vital that the information they provide is accurate, comprehensive, and free from bias (Grzanka & Frantell, 2017). Knowledge about abortion restrictions and the mental health impacts of such restrictions can help providers anticipate and treat issues that their clients may experience. Thus, providers should maintain an adequate understanding of the potential psychological effects an individual may experience either from having an abortion or from being unable to obtain an abortion and how these effects may impact people of diverse backgrounds (Landess et al., 2023). If referrals are needed, mental health professionals should also be informed about appropriate and accessible referral sources they can recommend to best help their clients.

Additionally, professionals must stay informed of ethical codes or laws that apply to the issue of reproductive rights to ensure they are practicing in both an ethical and a legal manner. This text should constitute only one of many evolving sources of information regarding one's professional responsibilities in this area. Providers should be familiar with the ethical standards and codes of the professional organizations to which they belong and which ethical standards/codes may be most relevant when it comes to issues of abortion or reproductive rights. Further, it is essential to know about existing and proposed legislation that may impact their clients or the work they do in the states in which they practice and, because this arena is evolving rapidly, keep up-to-date on changes in such legislation. Since mental health professionals may work with clients from different states over telehealth, it is important to be aware of how laws vary across states and the ethical and legal considerations of working across state lines (Baird & Mollen, 2023). As discussed in the chapter on laws, some of the legal issues mental health professionals may encounter involve limits on how they can assist clients interested in having abortions or mandatory reporting (particularly with regard to minors) of people who are considering or who have had abortions. Providers should also maintain awareness of ethical/legal decision-making models and how to handle potential conflicts between ethical codes and laws.

Part of staying informed includes knowing when an area is beyond one's scope of knowledge or expertise and therefore turning to others for advice or assistance. Consultation or supervision can help mental health professionals gain knowledge and skills, maintain ethical boundaries, receive emotional support, discuss challenges, and ultimately protect the well-being of those they serve (Millner & Hanks, 2002). Finally, because mental health professionals may not be well versed in legal matters, consultation with an attorney when there are questions about one's legal responsibilities is highly recommended.

Possessing Self-Awareness of Values and Biases

Another vital responsibility for mental health professionals is to engage in ongoing self-awareness of their values and biases when it comes to the topic of abortion. Mental health professionals, like most of the American population, are likely to have strong and deeply held personal views regarding abortion and related legislation. It is a topic that can be divisive and elicit powerful emotions. Thus, Millner and Hanks (2002) and Landess et al. (2023) have recommended that providers take steps toward increasing self-awareness as well as ensuring their own values/biases do not influence their clinical decisions. This can involve a thoughtful and thorough examination of one's moral and ethical views on abortion and how one may respond to clients discussing abortion-related issues (Millner & Hanks, 2002).

Specific ways of increasing self-awareness include training, supervision, and continuous self-monitoring to identify areas in need of further skill development (Landess et al., 2023). Mental health professionals must first recognize their preconceived notions about abortion and reproductive rights and then work to set aside these notions if they interfere with their ability to provide ethical and effective care to their clients. If a provider cannot do this, the responsible thing is to refer clients to someone who can (Rubin & Russo, 2004). Referrals too should reflect the client's, not the mental health professional's, values and needs, as the provider may be thought of as responsible for the quality of help that their clients receive from a referral source (Landess et al., 2023). Lastly, if mental health professionals themselves notice that they are experiencing intense distress related to working with clients who have abortion-related concerns or if abortion-related concerns are impacting their ability to practice effectively, they should actively seek their own counseling or other professional help (Landess et al., 2023).

Being Effective in Clinical Practice

In clinical practice, mental health professionals in a post-*Roe v. Wade* world can work to be effective in a multitude of ways. Clients may often need to work through issues related to abortion or abortion restrictions in a clinical setting. The professional's role is to be a support through it all, regardless of their personal views on the topic (Bray, 2018). Thus, as previously mentioned, of prime importance when working with people who have had an abortion, who are considering an abortion, or who are in any way impacted by abortion-related restrictions is setting aside one's personal opinions in the interest of best serving clients (Bray, 2018). Beyond abortion, reproductive rights may also be addressed in a clinical setting needing sensitive and ethical approaches to provide support for individuals as they navigate personal decisions related to contraception, fertility, and health care. The care provided to clients should never be aimed at a political agenda but instead must focus on each client's personal needs. No matter the professional's personal or moral views on abortion and reproductive rights, they must work to set these aside in clinical practice and remember their professional obligations to help and not harm.

Mental health professionals should utilize their skills of empathic listening, compassion, and nonjudgmental attitudes when considering each individual's unique story. They should be aware of how their verbal and nonverbal responses could impact their clients and strive to create a neutral and welcoming space where people feel comfortable discussing abortion-related issues (Bray, 2018). The mental health professional should also validate and normalize a range of cognitive and affective responses in their clients (Grzanka & Frantell, 2017). Professionals should be aware that lives are impacted not only by facing such sensitive matters personally and clinically but also by having to deal with them in a contentious social context and by navigating ever-changing laws impacting their options (Baird & Mollen, 2023).

Mental health professionals also need to be aware of unique concerns and special challenges when dealing with abortion- and reproductive rights-related issues in clinical practice, such as how intersectional identities can impact individuals post-*Roe v. Wade*. The issue of reproduction may require specific cultural sensitivities because of the ways that moral and religious values intersect with racial, socioeconomic, gender, and other identities (Rubin & Russo, 2004). The mental health professional should be able to capably work with individuals who are conflicted between their choices and their religious/spiritual beliefs. For example, people may choose abortion despite their religious beliefs espousing that abortion is wrong (Rubin & Russo, 2004). Mental health professionals should similarly be able to capably work with people who do not have such religious qualms about abortion but instead struggle with challenges related to access or discrimination.

Finally, as mentioned earlier, mental health professionals should understand the various considerations related to practicing in both an ethical and legal manner, many of which were described earlier in this text. Again, knowing the applicable laws in the states in which one practices is vital to ensure the actions a provider takes in their clinical practice are aboveboard. For example, in the context of confidentiality of records, there is a possibility that a mental health professional's records could be subpoenaed as evidence in abortion-related criminal or civil prosecution against a client or the professional (Baird & Mollen, 2023). Additionally, laws pertaining to minors, reproduction, and mental health care vary by state. Mental health professionals should therefore always address limits of confidentiality with clients at the beginning of treatment and as the need arises and consider what they choose to put in their records and how records are handled (Baird & Mollen, 2023). If professionals encounter any concerns related to their clinical practice in a post-*Roe v. Wade* world, consultation, supervision, and legal counsel, if necessary, are strongly recommended.

Self-Disclosure

Mental health professionals may wonder whether they should share their thoughts on abortion or on the overturning of *Roe v. Wade* with clients. In some cases, self-disclosure on the part of the provider can help clients feel more comfortable and can enhance the therapeutic relationship. Millner and Hanks (2002) and Landess et al. (2023) noted that disclosure on a mental health care provider's abortion stance is not necessarily verboten, but, if done, the provider should clearly state that their opinions or values are only their own and ensure that the disclosure is not interpreted as coercion in any way. The American Psychological Association (APA, 2022) agreed that the decision to self-disclose one's thoughts about abortion bans and related issues is personal, though they noted that withholding one's opinion from clients/patients may be the safest choice. That is, talking about one's personal views on such a sensitive topic may make the client/patient uncomfortable, particularly if they have differing values, could lead to clients/patients being unduly influenced by the provider, and could potentially incite complaints or even claims of negligence/malpractice. Ultimately, providers should remember that their professional obligation is to minimize harm and, if needed, utilize an ethical decision-making model and consultation/supervision to determine whether self-disclosure regarding personal views in this area is appropriate.

Countertransference

Countertransference, defined as the emotional responses of providers to their clients, can significantly impact the therapeutic relationship and the effectiveness of treatment. Research indicates that unmanaged countertransference can lead to negative feelings such as frustration, anger, and even therapeutic nihilism among providers (Lee, 2023; Hayes et al., 2018). These reactions not only affect the mental health professional's emotional well-being but can also compromise the therapeutic alliance and hinder the client's progress toward treatment goals (Pedhu, 2019; Hayes et al., 2018). For instance, when mental health professionals experience overwhelming emotions in response to a client's desire to have an abortion, it may lead to avoidance or inappropriate responses, ultimately damaging the therapeutic relationship (Fixsen et al., 2019; Gehlert et al., 2013). This vulnerability can stem from personal biases, discomfort with certain topics, or a lack of knowledge about abortion-related issues (Dictado & Torres-Harding, 2023; Cartwright et al., 2014). As a result, providers may inadvertently invalidate their clients' experiences or fail to provide the necessary support, which can exacerbate feelings of isolation or shame in clients discussing their issues or concerns (Abargil & Tishby, 2022; Hayes et al., 2015).

Effective management of countertransference is crucial for maintaining a healthy therapeutic environment. Strategies for managing countertransference reactions include self-reflection, supervision, and the use of mindfulness techniques (Guest & Carlson, 2019; Diener & Mesrie, 2015). Self-reflection allows mental health professionals to identify their emotional responses and understand how these may influence their clinical interactions with clients. Supervision provides a space to discuss experiences and receive feedback, which can enhance awareness and management of countertransference (Hayes et al., 2018). Mindfulness techniques, too, have been shown to help mental health professionals maintain a therapeutic presence and reduce negative emotional responses when working with challenging topics (Guest & Carlson, 2019). By creating a safe space for clients to discuss abortion-related concerns, mental health professionals can mitigate the impact of countertransference and enhance the therapeutic alliance (Pérez-Rojas et al., 2017; Hayes et al., 2018).

Case in Practice: Kevin

Many clinicians, like Florida psychotherapist Kevin, find themselves unprepared to navigate the intersection of ethical dilemmas, trauma, and systemic barriers that may arise in abortion-related cases. This unpreparedness not only compromises the therapeutic relationship but can also leave clients feeling overlooked or unsupported during their most vulnerable moments. Kevin's story is far from uncommon. During a session, a 23-year-old pregnant client confided to Kevin that she was not in a position to have a child and felt uncertain about her next steps. She revealed that she had been drugged and raped by a male co-worker but had not reported the assault to authorities, sharing her experience only with her best friend. The pregnancy came as a devastating shock, leaving her feeling powerless and trapped in a situation she never chose. She explained that since their state only permits abortion in cases of rape or incest, she was considering traveling out of state to access abortion services. However, she was adamant about not reporting the assault due to the deep shame she felt, believing she was partly to blame for being alone with her co-worker after hours. Adoption was not an option she could consider, as she said she could never "give a child away after carrying them for nine months." Her story highlights the emotional, physical, and systemic challenges faced by survivors of sexual assault in navigating reproductive decisions.

Kevin's professional training did not prepare him for this situation. He tried to support his client through the complexities of the case despite having little knowledge or training around the ethics and legalities surrounding his client's decision to terminate their pregnancy. He reported feeling inadequate when addressing her concerns and struggled with her decision to terminate the pregnancy due to his own beliefs. His feelings subconsciously impacted his interactions with the client in sessions, leading him to make unhelpful comments and provide substandard care. The client eventually left him for another therapist. We encourage readers to reflect upon the various ways Kevin could have improved his ability to effectively care for the client.

Abiding by Ethical Codes

This text has gone into great detail regarding ethics and how ethical codes/ standards may relate to issues of abortion and reproductive rights. It is incumbent upon mental health professionals to know the specific ethical code(s) that they are beholden to based on their degrees, licenses, and/or certifications. However, several ethical principles that have particular relevance to this topic are common across different professional ethical codes and are described below along with implications for professionals in clinical practice.

Autonomy is a principle of many ethical codes. The American Counseling Association (ACA, 2014) *Code of Ethics* describes autonomy as the right to control one's life. Mental health professionals in states with abortion bans may find it difficult to help foster clients' autonomy because, per Grzanka and Frantell (2017), abortion restrictions reinforce the idea that individuals cannot make responsible choices about their own bodies. An important implication for mental health professionals to respect client autonomy includes helping clients examine their choices and come to the best possible decision they can regarding abortion-related decisions without the professional imposing their own values on the client. Autonomy can be compromised by mental health professionals in cases where the provider's personal beliefs or values consciously or subconsciously affect the information or resources given to clients, thereby taking further control away from a client who may already feel like the Dobbs decision has impacted their autonomy.

Fidelity describes the essence of truthfulness within a relationship, leading to trust (ACA, 2014). In therapeutic relationships, trust is generally seen as essential. Fidelity can be challenged by abortion-related legislation in cases, for example, where mental health providers have to breach client confidentiality and report an individual's abortion to a parent/guardian or potentially authorities. As previously described, fidelity can be maintained through thorough and ongoing discussions with clients about the limits of confidentiality and how legislation impacts what they may share with others.

Justice, which refers to a sense of fairness, is another principle seen in many professional ethical codes. Concerning reproductive rights, mental health professionals may notice that legislation banning or limiting abortions unfairly impacts certain populations, such as people of color and people with low socioeconomic status. An implication for professionals to uphold this ethical principle is ensuring that the care they are providing to clients is fair/unbiased and accessible to all. Additionally, mental health professionals can engage in advocacy efforts and promote social justice through various activities, examples of which are described further in this chapter.

Several other common ethical principles may relate to the issues of abortion and reproductive rights. Beneficence, or acting in the best interest of others, implies that mental health professionals maintain knowledge and self-awareness to serve diverse groups of people who may be impacted by abortion-related laws in a manner that is best for the client, regardless of the professional's personal beliefs. Similarly, nonmaleficence, to "do no harm," may be seen as the flipside of beneficence (ACA, 2014). Mental health professionals may have differing thoughts on whether, who, and how much abortion and/or abortion-related laws harm various people (i.e., the fetus, the pregnant individual, and other family members). Again, mental health professionals must take steps not to impose their personal views on others and utilize consultation, supervision, and ethical decision-making models as appropriate when faced with ethical dilemmas.

Educating and Supervising Mental Health Professionals-in-Training

Mental health professionals-in-training who are working toward degrees, certifications, or licensure may turn to their instructors or supervisors for information or answers related to practicing in a post-Roe world. Educators or supervisors should proactively anticipate student/supervisee concerns and ensure they are able to either answer questions competently or direct them to appropriate resources that can. Educators should incorporate information about abortion-related matters and the provider's professional role into various courses. For example, courses on professional ethics may provide an opportunity for students to explore abortion-related issues, relevant ethical principles, and decision-making guidelines (Millner & Hanks, 2002). In both the classroom and the supervision room, educators and supervisors can help burgeoning mental health professionals engage in activities to assess their own potential biases when it comes to this subject, leading to greater self-awareness and making them better prepared to make sound ethical decisions concerning this issue with, perhaps, less personal distress (Millner & Hanks, 2002). Training and supervision efforts should ensure mental health professionals-in-training are equipped with the skills to engage in abortion-related discussions effectively, thereby reducing the likelihood of countertransference-related issues arising in practice (Dictado & Torres-Harding, 2023; Cartwright et al., 2014).

Contributing to Research

Mental health professionals should not only be informed about the impact of the overturning of *Roe v. Wade* and how it affects their clients and their practice but also be open to addressing and contributing to the empirical literature on such issues. Contributing to new research on the mental health effects of abortion restrictions is crucial for several reasons. First, it is essential to understand the psychological impact on individuals who are directly affected by restrictions on abortions, particularly among vulnerable or marginalized populations. As mentioned in the chapter on the mental health impacts of the ruling, there is currently a dearth of research in this area due to the recent nature of the ruling and the fact that abortion is stigmatized, meaning people may not come forward to participate in research, especially people who may have become pregnant due to rape or incest. However, this research is vital because identifying potential mental health challenges faced by various groups of people denied abortions can lead to targeted interventions to mitigate these effects. It can also provide a platform for the voices of diverse groups of people impacted by the ruling, ensuring their experiences and needs are recognized and addressed.

Second, studying the broader societal implications of the overturning of *Roe v. Wade* can inform policymakers and other key stakeholders about the potential mental health crisis that could arise, enabling them to allocate resources effectively, implement preventive measures, or pass legislation that is in the best interest of the public. Research can highlight the disparities in mental health outcomes among different demographic groups, leading to more equitable reproductive health care policies. Furthermore, understanding these mental health effects can contribute to public discourse, raising awareness about the importance of mental well-being in the context of legal and social changes surrounding reproductive rights.

Finally, research may further examine ethical and legal considerations for mental health professionals in a post-Roe world. Providers are likely to continue to face challenges and questions regarding their roles, and research can produce answers or help them understand effective ways to manage concerns or conflicts. Overall, research in this area is a step toward ensuring mental health support systems are equitable, inclusive, and responsive to the needs of all individuals, especially those who are most vulnerable, and toward providing mental health professionals with the necessary knowledge and tools to act in clients' best interests.

Engaging in Advocacy and Promoting Social Justice

In a call to action for counseling psychologists, Grzanka and Frantell (2017) argued that professionals should view themselves as integral to reproductive justice movements because of the field's focus on individual empowerment as well as its investment in social transformation. Further, they argued that mental health professionals have skills that can both address impediments to reproductive justice and promote sexual and reproductive health care as practitioners and advocates. Specifically, these professionals can become involved by challenging restrictive legislation, supporting individuals and families impacted by the laws, and empowering clients to advocate for themselves (Grzanka & Frantell, 2017). Baird and Mollen (2023) similarly called on mental health professionals to become politically and socially active to ensure the overall emotional and physical well-being of those who may be directly impacted by abortion-related legislation. Like Grzanka and Frantell (2017), Baird and Mollen (2023) noted the unique insights of providers and how their education and experience can be beneficial when speaking to legislators about mental health-related impacts and considerations.

Social and political advocacy efforts may also involve challenging abortion stigma. Abortion stigma refers to the culturally pervasive ways in which abortion and those who have abortions are devalued, marginalized, and pathologized. It is considered a concealable stigma that is unknown to others unless otherwise disclosed (Grzanka & Frantell, 2017). Mental health professionals can work to address and oppose such stigmas that can harm clients. Stigma-challenging advocacy initiatives may include education and awareness campaigns, language and terminology review (i.e., promoting respectful language and actively discouraging the use of stigmatizing terms related to abortion in professional literature), policy advocacy (i.e., supporting policies that combat abortion stigma), and organizing events and activities that foster dialogue and understanding within the community.

Finally, since abortion-related bans disproportionately impact people of marginalized groups, such as women, people of color, and people living in poverty, social justice advocacy is inherently a part of reproductive rights advocacy. Mental health professionals should acknowledge clients' multidimensional identities and consider dimensions of privilege and oppression (Grzanka & Frantell, 2017). Their advocacy efforts should address the particular challenges of marginalized groups and aim to create a fairer society where everyone has equal access to opportunities and is treated with dignity, regardless of their background or identity. Social justice advocacy can also amplify the voices of the underrepresented people impacted by abortion bans and work to dismantle oppressive structures that disproportionately affect marginalized communities.

Conclusion

In conclusion, the overturning of *Roe v. Wade* has presented complex challenges and responsibilities for mental health professionals that span across legal, ethical, and social justice domains. This text has provided an in-depth analysis of these multifaceted implications, highlighting the critical roles clinicians must play in adapting their practice to meet the evolving needs of their clients. Key steps include maintaining ongoing awareness of legislative changes, possessing self-awareness regarding one's own biases and values, ensuring that ethical considerations guide practice, and fostering an inclusive environment that respects diverse perspectives on reproductive rights. Additionally, education and supervision practices must be updated to equip emerging professionals with the skills necessary to navigate these challenges effectively. Research efforts should be directed toward understanding the broader psychological impacts of such legal changes to inform evidence-based practices. Finally, mental health professionals are called to advocate for policies that protect reproductive rights and promote mental well-being, reinforcing their commitment to social justice. By addressing these areas, mental health professionals can uphold their ethical obligations while providing comprehensive support to those affected by these significant legal shifts.

Discussion Questions

1) Reflect on your own personal thoughts and beliefs related to abortion. How do you think these thoughts and beliefs developed?
2) Do you think you can set aside your personal thoughts and beliefs related to abortion for ethical practice? How would you do this?
3) How can mental health professionals communicate with legislators on topics related to reproductive rights?
4) What kinds of advocacy efforts could you become involved in related to reproductive rights and serving in your clients'/patients' best interests?

References

Abargil, M., & Tishby, O. (2022). Countertransference awareness and treatment outcome. *Journal of Counseling Psychology, 69*(5), 667–677. https://doi.org/10.1037/cou0000620

American Counseling Association. (2014). *2014 ACA code of ethics.* https://www.counseling.org/knowledge-center/ethics

American Psychological Association. (2022). *Abortion [FAQ].* https://www.apa.org/topics/abortion

Baird, B. N., & Mollen, D. (2023). *The internship, practicum, and field placement handbook: A guide for the helping professions* (9th ed.). Routledge. https://doi.org/10.4324/9781003325697

Bray, B. (2018, April 03). When post-abortion emotions need unpacking. *Counseling Today.* https://ct.counseling.org/2018/04/when-post-abortion-emotions-need-unpacking/

Cartwright, C., Rhodes, P., King, R., & Shires, A. (2014). Experiences of countertransference: Reports of clinical psychology students. *Australian Psychologist, 49*(4), 232–240. https://doi.org/10.1111/ap.12062

Dictado, J., & Torres-Harding, S. (2023). Predictors of therapy trainees' pathologizing and invalidating microaggressions with sexual and racial minority therapy clients. *Training and Education in Professional Psychology, 17*(3), 304–313. https://doi.org/10.1037/tep0000424

Diener, M., & Mesrie, V. (2015). Supervisory process from a supportive–expressive relational psychodynamic approach. *Psychotherapy, 52*(2), 153–157. https://doi.org/10.1037/a0038085

Fixsen, A., Ridge, D., & Evans, C. (2019). 'Momma bear wants to protect': Vicarious parenting in practitioners working with disturbed and traumatised children. *Counselling and Psychotherapy Research, 20*(4), 680–688. https://doi.org/10.1002/capr.12285

Gehlert, K., Pinke, J., & Segal, R. (2013). A trainee's guide to conceptualizing countertransference in marriage and family therapy supervision. *The Family Journal, 22*(1), 7–16. https://doi.org/10.1177/1066480713504894

Grzanka, P. R., & Frantell, K. A. (2017). Counseling psychology and reproductive justice: A call to action. *The Counseling Psychologist, 45*(3), 326–352. https://doi.org/10.1177/0011000017699871

Guest, J., & Carlson, R. (2019). Utilizing mindfulness strategies to manage negative countertransference and feelings of dislike while working with children exhibiting externalized behaviors. *Journal of Psychotherapy Integration, 29*(4), 426–439. https://doi.org/10.1037/int0000183

Hayes, J., Gelso, C., Goldberg, S., & Kivlighan, D. (2018). Countertransference management and effective psychotherapy: Meta-analytic findings. *Psychotherapy, 55*(4), 496–507. https://doi.org/10.1037/pst0000189

Hayes, J., Nelson, D., & Fauth, J. (2015). Countertransference in successful and unsuccessful cases of psychotherapy. *Psychotherapy, 52*(1), 127–133. https://doi .org/10.1037/a0038827

Landess, J., Hatters-Friedman, S., Kaempf, A., & Ross, N. (2023). Abortion and the psychiatrist: Practicing in post-Dobbs America. *The Psychiatric Times, 40*(1). https://www.psychiatrictimes.com/view/abortion-and-the-psychiatrist-practicing -in-post-dobbs-america

Lee, W. (2023). Personal growth experiences of countertransference among Malaysian counsellors: A phenomenological study. *Journal of Health and Translational Medicine, 26*(1), 96–104. https://doi.org/10.22452/jummec.vol26no1.15

Millner, V. S., & Hanks, R. B. (2002). Induced abortion: an ethical conundrum for counselors. *Journal of Counseling & Development, 80*, 57–63. https://doi-org .tcsedsystem.idm.oclc.org/10.1002/j.1556-6678.2002.tb00166.x

Pedhu, Y. (2019). Efforts to overcome countertransference in pastoral counseling relationships. *Journal of Pastoral Care & Counseling Advancing Theory and Professional Practice Through Scholarly and Reflective Publications, 73*(2), 74–81. https://doi.org/10.1177/1542305019852587

Pérez-Rojas, A., Palma, B., Bhatia, A., Jackson, J., Norwood, E., Hayes, J., & Gelso, C. (2017). The development and initial validation of the countertransference management scale. *Psychotherapy, 54*(3), 307–319. https://doi.org/10.1037/ pst0000126

Rubin, L., & Russo, N. F. (2004). Abortion and mental health: What therapists need to know. *Women & Therapy, 27*(3–4), 69–90. https://doi.org/10.1300/J015v27n03_06